Eating Grass, Drinking Wine

Eating Grass, Drinking Wine

Liyan Liu

HAMILTON BOOKS
Lanham • Boulder • New York • London

Published by Hamilton Books
An imprint of The Rowman & Littlefield Publishing Group, Inc.
4501 Forbes Boulevard, Suite 200, Lanham, Maryland 20706
www.rowman.com

6 Tinworth Street, London SE11 5AL, United Kingdom

British Library Cataloguing in Publication Information Available

Library of Congress Cataloging-in-Publication Data

Library of Congress Control Number: 2020951547

∞™ The paper used in this publication meets the minimum requirements of American National Standard for Information Sciences—Permanence of Paper for Printed Library Materials, ANSI/NISO Z39.48-1992.

Contents

List of Illustrations   vii

Part I: Eating Grass

Chapter One: Burning Down the House   3

Chapter Two: Red Paper Flowers   13

Chapter Three: I'm Leaving   25

Chapter Four: The Little Match-Seller   37

Chapter Five: Poison Ivy   41

Chapter Six: A Drop of Blood   47

Chapter Seven: A Single Plank   61

Part II: Drinking Wine

Chapter Eight: A Touch of Elegance   69

Chapter Nine: A Raincoat Made of Straw   77

Chapter Ten: The Pride of Heaven   87

Chapter Eleven: A Wild, Vast Moor   93

Chapter Twelve: Guardian Angel   103

Chapter Thirteen: Guests in this World   115

Epilogue   127

About the Author   129

List of Illustrations

Illustration 1. Watercolor painting of Great Grandfather walking slowly in the backyard garden with a pear in hand by Liu Shuyong, pen name 老树画画 (laoshu huahua). He is the dean and a professor of the School of Culture and Media, Central University of Finance and Economics. He is well known for his unique paintings which blend modern and traditional cultures in artistic form. All of his paintings accompany short poems for explanatory purposes. Here is the poem for this painting.

持梨小园闲走，
花儿开上心头。
千古浑如一梦，
此生却多离愁。

Wandering the backyard pear in hand,
My heart brightens like blossoms land.
Thousand years of the same dream,
Only my tearful farewells never end.

This poem was translated into English by Aiguo Han, Professor of Writing at Rowan University

Illustration 2. 河南大学校门 Color photograph of Henan University Entrance, which was built in 1935. Credit: Archives of the University History, Henan University.

Illustration 3. 河南大学曾用图书馆 Color photograph of Henan University's former Library. This building, built in 1915, was the first building on campus. It integrated traditional Chinese and Western architectural styles in its design. Credit: Archives of the University History, Henan University.

Illustration 4. 河南大学曾用阅览室 Color photograph of Henan University's former Research & Resource Center, which was built in 1921. Credit: Archives of the University History, Henan University.

Illustration 5. Color photograph of Georgetown College's Learning Resource Center. Credit: Georgetown College stock photo.

Illustration 6. Color photograph of The Ohio State University's University Hall. Credit: The Ohio State University.

Illustration 7. Watercolor painting of a raincoat made of straw by Liu Shuyong, pen name 老树画画 (laoshu huahua). Here is the poem for this painting.

一身躬耕田亩，
不与世人纷争。
山中一簑烟雨，
自在但任平生。

The land is all I attend,
No need to argue with man.
Old straw raincoat and mountain rain,
I am myself beginning or end.

This poem was translated into English by Aiguo Han, Professor of Writing at Rowan University

Illustration 8. Color photograph of IUP Oak Grove. Credit: Keith Boyer/ Indiana University of Pennsylvania.

Illustration 9. Color photograph of the Statue of Liberty. Credit: William T. McCabe.

I

EATING GRASS

CHAPTER ONE

Burning Down the House

My maternal grandmother's parents died very young. In fact, Grandmother only had one memory of her father, when she was quite young. They lived in a family compound with a beautiful garden. I can never forget the story Grandmother said:

> When I was about four years old, one late summer day I was with my father in our backyard garden. The air was hot and damp, and dark clouds scowled overhead, but my father did not mind any of this. He was slowly walking in the backyard garden, and picked a pear from the pear tree.
> 'May I have some of your pear?' I asked.
> 'Of course.' My father smiled and gave me a bite of the pear.
> But my grandma was also there, and she scowled at my father. 'What are you doing? These pears are for curing your disease! If she wants to eat some pears, there are plenty inside!'

According to traditional Chinese medicine, pears help to balance the lungs and improve their function, so I think my great-grandfather must have had some kind of lung disease such as tuberculosis. And soon after that he died.

Grandmother also only had one memory of her mother, and I think it must have been soon after Great-grandfather died. Great-grandmother was sitting on the stairs outside the gated entrance to the family compound, between the stone guardian lion statues. A strong, dry autumn breeze was blowing from the north. She was holding Grandmother in her arms, and crying. Several other people were there, trying to comfort her.

"For the sake of the child you must go on living," someone said.

Great-grandmother replied, "If only I had a boy, I could go on living."

"It is better to have a boy," said someone else. "Girls are useless."

"But it is not the child's fault she is a girl," the first person replied. "And without girls to become women, there would be no boys."

"She became a woman, and there is still no boy," said the second person.

3

Figure 1.1.   Watercolor painting of Great Grandfather walking slowly in the backyard garden with a pear in hand by Liu Shuyong pen name 老树画画 （laoshu huahua). From Liu Shuyong, 老树画画 （laoshu huahua)

Great-grandmother sobbed and ran into the house, leaving Grand-mother behind, and soon after that, Great-grandmother killed herself.

Grandmother had no siblings, so her grandma was the only family she had left. They continued to live together in the big family compound, but her grandma did not really care about her. Grandmother slept with her wet nurse every night until she was six or seven years old. But the wet nurse did not care about her either. They were not close, and the wet nurse did not even allow Grandmother to touch her at night or sleep close to her.

Several years later the wet nurse went home to give birth to a baby. She was gone for several months, and when she returned, Grandmother did not want her any more.

"Why did you come back?" she said. "I am too old to need a wet nurse. And you do not care about me anyway. I could have slept with a rock in my bed and not noticed the difference."

The wet nurse burst into tears and ran out of the house.

So Grandmother grew into a woman with only her grandma living in the house. Of course, they had a few maids and cooks. And although she became a very beautiful woman, she had few friends and no one wanted to marry her. People believed that her fate was too hard, as though she were cursed. They were afraid to get close to her. It was not until she was 27 years old that she met Grandfather, and since he had also lost both parents, he accepted her. She became He Zhang Shi, which is the tradi-tional way to refer to married women; He was her husband's surname, Zhang was hers, and Shi was the equivalent of Mrs. I do not know her given name.

My maternal grandfather, born He Xin Fu, was the youngest child of his parents; he had one elder brother and two elder sisters. His parents must been in their 40s when he was born. As was the custom among educated gentry or elite families, they gave him the courtesy name of He Song Jun. So that was what his peers called him, while his elders used his birth name. His father was a well-regarded private tutor who traveled to Japan to give lectures, and taught children of high ranking officials from all over north central China. Grandfather was fortunate enough that his father sometimes brought him to Japan. It was all part of his education and training, so that he could become a scholar like his father. Grandfa-ther's elder brother became Henan Province's Minister of Posts and Com-munications, responsible for mail transport, telegraph communications, and the rail network. His two sisters married two high ranking military officers, and left home at that time to live with their husbands. And his parents died young, so eventually the only people left at home with Grandfather were his sister-in-law and her two sons. Grandfather and his two nephews were actually about the same age, and they did not get along. Sometimes they got into fights, and of course his sister-in-law was unhappy about that. She blamed him for the fights, refusing to believe that her sons could be troublemakers.

It all got worse when he married. His sister-in-law did not like Grandmother, and blamed her for every bit of bad luck. One day she came home from the market to find a chair had been broken. She rushed to find Grandfather, shouting "Where are you, you hoodlum?"

Of course, he did not like being called a hoodlum. "Who are you to call me names in my own house?" he shouted back.

"Your house?" she spat back, her face red with anger. "This is your elder brother's house now! He is a respectable man, and you shame him with your behavior. Does not Kongzi say, 'The strength of a nation derives from the integrity of the home'?"

"When anger rises, think of the consequences," he replied, quoting Confucius right back at her.

"What you do not want done to yourself, do not do to others," she replied with another quote.

"Silence is a true friend who never betrays." With that, he turned his back on her.

"To see and listen to the wicked is already the beginning of wickedness," she shouted at his back, then turned and stormed away.

When Grandfather awoke the following morning, his sister-in-law and her sons were gone—he was alone in the house. He felt betrayed and abandoned, and was never much angrier in his life. He said to himself, "This house is cursed, and no one should live here," so in his fury, he burned down the house. I say house, but in Western terms I should call it a compound, since it had multiple buildings and a wall around it. This has been common throughout much of China's history. For instance, even in the Neolithic age, as early as in Yangshao Stage (5000-3000 BC), the Yangshao people lived in villages and each village was often surrounded by a wall or a ditch which separated the village from the area in which the dead were buried. This tradition continues till today. Today in China every city, neighborhood, school, hospital, factory, and place of work is still surrounded by a wall.

They lived in Kaifeng, the capital city of Henan Province at that time, but now Grandfather had no family nearby and no home. As his anger cooled, he realized what a foolish thing he had done. *It is like Lao Tzu says,* he thought, *"Violence, even well intentioned, always rebounds upon oneself."* And he asked himself, *Who can I turn to now? Who will help a fool?*

Now, when Grandfather was a boy, one of his father's other pupils was Wu Peifu, who became the most prominent general during China's Warlord Era. They grew very close in the course of their studies, and even became sworn brothers. In Chinese culture, becoming sworn brothers is a much bigger deal than what it means to be blood brothers in America. They went to a temple to conduct the ritual. They lit incense, and swore an oath that they would always help and be loyal to each other. They burnt a paper with the oath and their names written on it, so that their oath would forever be stored in the celestial archives. The oath said, "We could not be born the same year, the same month, and the same day, but shall die the same year, the same month, and the same day." And they shared a meal. During the meal, each one cut his finger, and—instead of joining the fingers together as is the American custom—mixed his blood into a glass of wine. Then after the meal they and all the witnesses drank from the wine.

"With such a bond between us," Grandfather said to Grandmother, "let us hope he is willing to help."

So they decided to go west to Wu's headquarters in Luoyang. With European help, the Qing government had built a railway fifteen years earlier between Kaifeng and Luoyang, but Grandfather and Grandmother could not afford the train, so they traveled by boat instead.

They boarded a boat for the 150 mile journey up the Yellow River to the Yiluo River, and from there to Luoyang. It was early summer, and with snowmelt from Mongolia and rainfall from the mountains, the river was running high. The lower stretch of this river is known, in fact, for being "above ground." This is possible because, to try to protect against the massive floods the Yellow River is prone to, levees have been built over the centuries—but because the river deposits so much silt, it fills up the river bed and the surface of the water rises above the ground level of the surrounding land. So as the boat sailed along, sail taut from the typical warm moist breeze from the southeast, they could look out over the fertile fields of wheat and sesame. They could not help thinking of the fact that this river and the land around it had been one of the ancient cradles of Chinese civilization.

Late on the third day, the boat turned southwest and followed the Yiluo River upstream. Early afternoon the following day, as they approached the confluence of the Yi and Luo Rivers, which combined to form the Yiluo, they gazed reverentially toward the distant Mount Song, one of the Five Great Mountains sacred in Chinese traditional religion, and home to the Shaolin Monastery traditionally considered the birthplace of Zen Buddhism.

At the end of the fourth day of travel, the boat reached Luoyang. Disembarking on the north side of the river, Grandfather asked a passerby where they could find General Wu.

"Follow this road to the Lijing Gate, and ask the soldiers there. They will know," the man replied.

So Grandfather and Grandmother made their way through the riverside shops and houses till they came to a gatehouse in an imposing watchtower. The well-dressed, alert guards were hard to miss in their light blue uniforms, the white cloth wrapped around their calves shining in the bright sunlight. They barked directions to General Wu's office.

As my grandparents followed the directions, they were struck by how different Luoyang felt, despite being, like Kaifeng, one of the ancient capitals of China—and both in Henan Province. Red lanterns decorated the bustling shopping streets and residential alleys, and the distinctive appearance of the Moslem Hui people who had lived in Luoyang for a thousand years was outdone by the exotic aroma from their restaurants. Even the conversations of the Chinese they passed sounded odd, as the Luoyang dialect, while close to the general Henan dialect they spoke, was different enough to be noticeable.

When they turned on to the street they had been told Wu's office was on, it did not look any different from the others.

"Shouldn't a general work with the troops he commands?" asked Grandmother suspiciously. "Why does he have an office in the city?"

"General Wu is an important man!" Grandfather replied. "He is not just a general—he is the High Inspecting Commissioner of five provinces! He is working hard to promote a new constitution for China. And anyway, there has not been any fighting since last year."

"Why do they fight so much? It just makes life worse for everyone else."

Grandfather chuckled. "I suspect that if you asked each of the warlords, and listened to his reply, you would still not know the answer. They are complex men, and while desire for power is undoubtedly one reason, Wu for one seems to have China's best interests at heart, so he feels he must fight those who do not."

Grandmother harrumphed. "How can a warlord know what is best for the people?"

"My father taught him—"

"The same as he taught you? You burned down your own house."

Grandfather was silent for a moment. "Wu is much more than a warlord. He is known as a philosopher. He studies agriculture, poetry, and art, and when he trains soldiers he teaches them literature as well."

"Well, a superior man exceeds in his actions," said Grandmother, referring to a Confucius quote. "I hope his actions toward you are just."

Grandfather knocked on the door, which bore a simple sign saying only, "General Wu Peifu."

A soldier opened the door and stood in the doorway, eyeing them with a prompting expression.

"I am He Song Jun, sworn brother of General Wu, and I am in need of his assistance," Grandfather announced.

The soldier bowed and ushered them inside. "Please wait here," he said, indicating a bench in the small waiting room, which was tastefully decorated with a modern flair. Before they had time to sit down, he had returned and was motioning for them to follow him.

General Wu Peifu was a man of average height, balding with brownish buzz-cut hair on the sides and back of his head—and just a hint of grey. Unusually for a Chinese, his alert eyes were light brown and his mustache was almost ginger in color. He was standing near the entrance to his office, and greeted them on sight with the fist-and-palm salute.

Grandfather returned the greeting, while Grandmother bowed to him. He gestured to them to sit, and they noted the two steaming cups of tea already waiting for them. He carried himself in a commanding, slightly haughty manner, but the expression on his face was welcoming.

"Too many years have passed since I had the pleasure of your company," he said. "It is good to see you have married." Once they had sat down, he seated himself. They were distracted by the large portrait hanging on the wall behind him, of an elderly noble-looking Westerner.

"George Washington," he said with respect. "The American general who became the first leader of the new country. He stepped down as President so others could lead peacefully after him—an example some in China would do well to follow. But you have not come to discuss him."

"Thank you for your hospitality," Grandfather said, bowing his head. "You have many more important matters to attend to."

Wu shook his head. "What can be more important than a sworn brother in need? Now, tell me what has happened."

Grandfather sipped his tea, then began the story. He told it without relish or embellishment, and hung his head in shame when he came to burning down his house.

"What have you learned from this?" asked Wu when Grandfather came to the end.

"That I am a foolish man who must never decide in anger."

"The faults of a superior person are like the sun and moon. They have their faults, and everyone sees them; they change and everyone looks up to them."

Grandfather nodded in recognition of the Confucius quote.

Wu stood and began pacing. "Though you are a learned scholar, you know nothing of military or political matters. It is difficult to see how you could be of value in my affairs."

Grandfather lowered his head. "A poor scholar is never of value in violent times."

Wu nodded sympathetically. "Alas, in times of war even a wise man must fight, or no one will listen. However," he stopped pacing, "that does not mean I cannot help you." Reaching in to a pocket, he withdrew a key and unlocked the bottom drawer of his desk. He counted out a hundred silver Yuan Shikai dollar coins, then called for his assistant to fetch a bag.

"Use this money to start a business here in Luoyang. Choose a modest commodity that people need in peace as well as in war. Aim to make a living, not enrich yourself."

Grandfather and grandmother both rose and bowed deeply. "You are too generous," said Grandfather.

Wu waved his hand dismissively. "My accomplishments would count for nothing if I did not come to the aid of my sworn brother."

The assistant returned and handed an embroidered cloth bag to Wu. The coins tinkled as Wu scooped them into it.

Grandfather did not know what to say, but his gratitude was clear. He bowed again as Wu offered him the heavy bag.

As they stepped back out into the street, Grandfather weighed the bag in his hand. "What do you think now," he asked, "did he exceed in his actions?"

"Who can put a price on the bond between sworn brothers?" Grandmother replied. "If he trains his own soldiers in literature, I fail to see why you could not have assisted him. But he did help you, and one hundred silver dollars is certainly enough to go into business with."

And so Grandfather did, despite what it meant for his social station. Back then China had four social classes, with scholars at the top and merchants at the bottom. Those who became scholars did not learn practical skills; Grandfather had only one, repairing damage to ancient books and paintings, and during that war-filled time in China, there was very little demand for it.

But he had to do something. So even though he had always looked down on merchants, he used his *guanxi*, his personal connections (the "back door"), to get a contract providing clothing to the provincial government. Grandfather was a poor businessman, and did not manage to make a living and provide for the family that soon grew. General Wu, known as the "Jade Marshal," was the subject of Time Magazine's cover article on September 8, 1924—they called him the "biggest man in China"—but by 1927 the Kuomintang had grown strong enough to defeat him, and he fled to Sichuan. Any hope of further help from him was gone.

Grandfather and Grandmother lived in Luoyang for the rest of their lives. Grandfather eventually got a job teaching at Luoyang Number One Senior High School, which was—and is—one of the best high schools in the province. As an adjunct instructor, he only taught a few classes, and did not make much money. The family slipped into genteel poverty even before the Communists took over. The family business, which never really thrived, suffered a mortal blow in 1953 when the Communists moved the capital of Henan from Kaifeng to Zhengzhou. He lost his back door into provincial politics, and the business failed.

Grandfather never did have any more contact with the rest of his family. Mother remembers that when she was little, letters would arrive from her aunts, but Grandfather never replied to them. And while his motivation was personal, it worked out well for us under the Communists, because in the 1950s he began to read in the *People's Daily* that some of his family members were being put in prison, or even executed. Mother remembered that one day in 1952, Grandfather had pointed out the name, He Dasheng, in the newspaper as someone who had been arrested that day as a "Bad Element," or enemy of the people. He said to Mother:

"He was my nephew, and your cousin."

The original family of Grandfather were seen as belonging to particularly bad classes of people, and if Grandfather had had any contact with them, he and his family would have been under suspicion too.

As it was, while the fact that they were merchants did mark them as capitalists, their poverty spared them any real punishment. They had to study Mao Zedong Thought and write self-criticisms, but then they were considered redeemed and allowed to work in a small cooperative producing the clothing they had been selling.

Mother never knew anything about Grandfather's old family until they appeared in the newspaper. Then he finally told her about them. It was a terrible way to learn about one's family, and in her turn, Mother didn't tell me about it until I was in my twenties. I joked with her that it felt like my whole family were bad guys, but I really was shocked.

I am the oldest of four children, born in the spring of 1957; China's one-child policy did not start until 1979. My brother was born seven years after me, and my oldest sister was born twelve years later. At that time, the Chinese government assigned each person to a job, and they often separated couples. So my mother was assigned to a factory in Luoyang where we lived, but my father was assigned to Beijing. All my father could do to support his family was to send some money, but no one in China made much money back then. We saw him for two weeks every year when he used his visiting relatives leave; Mother got to see him more because she would use her leave to visit him. But we did not really have a father, and Mother was effectively what we would now call a single mother.

My grandmother lived with us when I was very young, and took care of me while Mother worked. This was a common arrangement because there were no private daycares for children, and while some *danwei* (working unit/place) had nurseries or kindergarten-type facilities, ours did not. Then she went to live with my uncle (her son) and his family, and I missed her terribly. When my brother was born, I became the second mother, and continued to do that when my sisters were born. The factory gave Mother one hour for lunch time, and in that hour she rushed home and prepared lunch for us. But then there was no time for her to eat anything, so she would bring some steamed bread to eat as she hurried back to work.

I always had a good memory, and learned to read at an early age. Later on I asked Mother, "How did I learn to read so early?"

"Whenever you saw a word you didn't know," she said, "you just asked me what it was. You always remembered my answers, so you learned quickly."

By the time I was five years old, I could already read high-school level books. When I had time, I would visit my neighbors, often while they were cooking.

"Can I read a story to you?" I would ask them, but they just ignored me. I would start to read out loud to them anyway; I thought that they were just unhappy because their children were about my age but could not read yet.

Being able to read so early did not help me when I started school. The teacher would write a new word on the blackboard, and I would speak up immediately, saying the word and what it meant.

One day the teacher talked to me after class. "You mustn't do that," she said. "You must let me teach the pronunciation and meaning of the words."

So I stopped. But then I didn't learn anything for the first two years.

Mother was pregnant when we received a note one night that Grandmother was dying. We took a bus and hurried to be with her. She was alone in her old house, with only a candle for light because her old house had no electricity. According to Chinese tradition, when you were pregnant you should not attend a funeral, or even go into the room where a loved one died, to protect the baby from negativity and spirits. So Mother had to stay in another room while I went in by myself to be with Grandmother. I called out the name we used for her, Lao Lao. I could hear Mother outside beginning to cry. Although it was night and I was alone with a dying woman, I was not afraid. Grandmother did not respond to anything I said. Finally she closed her eyes and passed away.

I cleaned her face and body, combed her hair, and changed her clothes; she had followed tradition and prepared a set of new clothes to wear for her journey to the next world. She had been a second mother to me, often taking care of me because Mother was so busy. I loved and missed Grandmother so much. I wanted to draw her pictures because she did not have any pictures left of us. I could see her in my dreams until a few months later, when her appearance was erased from my mind; even today I can't think of what she looked like.

CHAPTER TWO

Red Paper Flowers

One morning near the end of my second grade school year, I arrived at school (which of course had a wall around it) to find the gate shut. As usual, I was the first one there. The two Yulan magnolia trees on either side of the gate were covered in white flowers, and the smell of them always made me want to eat an orange, but I quickly forgot about that when I got close enough to see the sign hanging on the gate that said the school was closed. I did not know what to do. Why was the school closed?

"So it's true!" I heard a voice behind me, along with slapping footsteps. I turned to see it was the boy we called Big Nose.

"What's true?" I asked.

"Mother said school would be closed," said Big Nose. "But I had to see for myself. Long Live Chairman Mao!"

"Why would Chairman Mao close our school?"

"It's not just our school, it's all schools."

"But he says that 'an army without culture is a dull-witted army, and a dull-witted army cannot defeat the enemy.'" I protested. *Quotations from Chairman Mao Zedong*, usually referred to in the West as the "Little Red Book," had been published and widely distributed the year before, and I had read it several times.

Due to our bad background, my family did not have access to the best sources of news like Big Nose's family had. His parents were both factory workers—a very respectable background—and not only was his mother a cadre, she was the Party Secretary for the factory. So he usually knew what was really going on. He said you couldn't just read the newspaper, that it was like a code you could only interpret if you knew the context.

"But not old culture. Old culture is bad, and that's what our schools are teaching us. They are all bourgeois. We are starting a new revolution to remove capitalists and revisionists from society. It is the Great Proletarian Cultural Revolution!"

"If what our teachers have been teaching us is bad culture, then what is good culture?" I asked.

He wrinkled his sizable nose in puzzlement. "I don't know."

"Now we are not learning anything at all."

My best friend Miao Jianxiu ran up, yelling "Why is school closed?" Although she was named after Hao Jianxiu—a national model worker from Qingdao who had pioneered a number of innovations for cotton mills and was now deputy head of one—her uncle had worked for a British company before Liberation, so like mine, her family was suspect.

"So we can get rid of capitalist roaders like you," shouted Big Nose.

I grabbed Jianxiu's hand and ran off to get her away from him. "I'll try to explain later," I said.

Despite his mother's access to inside information, Big Nose was too young to understand the full picture. The Party had been moving in this direction for years, but not until May, 1966, did it officially decide that traditional education encouraged class division because it was tailored to the middle and upper classes. And because many in China's intelligentsia at that time had been educated in the West, they were considered the product of a bourgeois society. So, no school for anyone.

Some of my friends joined the Little Red Guards, which was for primary school students who were too young to join the Red Guards officially (though some did anyway). I felt lucky that my family's background did not cause us much trouble; I had friends whose families were torn apart due to their backgrounds. Because Chairman Mao supported the growth of the Red Guard movement, I wanted very much to join, but was never able to. The Sixteen Articles that defined what the Cultural Revolution was about were very clear that persuasion, not force, was how change was to be made, yet many of the Red Guards I saw were violent and sometimes even brutal. And in the early years most of them were children of high ranking Party leaders. I did not like what I saw them doing. It was all such a profound inversion of Chinese values. Others have written very effectively about that part of the Cultural Revolution, so I do not feel the need to.

Anyway, for almost a year and a half, I spent all day wandering around and playing outside with my friends, day after day.

We were called back to school late in 1967, but it was very different. Our school was assigned to a large factory nearby, which sent a Worker Propaganda Team to run the school. They conducted Mao-think classes and self-criticism sessions to reform the school. We learned politics from members of the army, mathematics from factory accountants, and industrial knowledge from factory workers, agricultural knowledge from farmers, and revolutionary literature and art from those of our teachers who had demonstrated their loyalty to Chairman Mao and were allowed to stay. It was all about putting the proletariat in charge and molding the students into good revolutionaries. We spent a lot of time chanting slogans, many of which were about Mao, like "Chairman Mao is the red sun in our hearts," and "Boundlessly loyal to the great leader Chairman Mao, boundlessly loyal to the great Mao Zedong Thought, boundlessly loyal to Chairman Mao's revolutionary line."

Even though primary and secondary schools were open again, universities and colleges remained shut down. This left millions of young people with nothing to do, which made an existing problem worse. In 1966, the Party began the "Up to the Mountains, Down to the Countryside" program, which called for educated young people to leave the big cities and participate in agricultural production in the countryside. At that time it was intended to address the problem of urban unemployment. These educated urban young people sent to rural areas became known as *zhishi qingnian* ("educated youth" or "sent-down youth,")—or *zhiqing* for short.

In December 1968, faced with so many idle youths, an article in the People's Daily included this quote from Chairman Mao:

> It is necessary for Educated Youth to go to the countryside and get re-educated by poor and lower-middle class peasants. We should persuade urban cadres and other people to send their children who are graduates of junior and senior high schools and universities to the countryside, to carry out the mobilization.
>
> Comrades in various rural areas should welcome them.

This instruction added an ideological motivation for sending *zhiqing* out to do manual labor with the peasants, and the government turned that into a patriotic campaign.

Soon after that, youths from all cities and towns were being sent out. I was not old enough at that time, but in school we were learning the skills we would need, and we began to spend half the school year working, either in the communes alongside peasants during harvest season, or in the factories alongside workers. This experience would prepare us to be sent to the countryside when we were old enough.

In my sixth grade year, primary school was changed from six years to five years, so both fifth and sixth graders graduated from primary school at the end of that year. Since we were not receiving an education that progressively built on what was learned each year, the fifth graders didn't have any difficulty making the jump to seventh grade. We all mixed together as classmates in middle school, but that seventh grade class was enormous—about a thousand students.

By that point, most of our former teachers had left as a result, directly and indirectly, of the "re-education" they had experienced in the last few years. Most of them wanted to prove that they could transform themselves into revolutionaries, some because they genuinely desired it, and some simply to survive. The two paths to transformation were either to be criticized and repudiated by the student body, or to integrate with the peasants in the countryside or with the workers in the factories – and it was made clear that the ultimate demonstration of loyalty to Chairman Mao would be the desire to do the latter. So many of our teachers asked to be sent out because it seemed less painful than the mass criticism. We did not know what it was really like to live in the countryside; all we knew was that the Party made it seem glorious.

So all through the four years of middle school and the two years of high school, we dedicated ourselves to becoming good revolutionaries, learning skills, and working. During high school we only received about two months of classroom time in two year. Then it turned out that just being old enough (the age of eligibility had been set at 16 in 1963, but many younger children were sent) did not guarantee we could go. Some of us, including me, were "permitted" to continue our education and were not sent out to the countryside with the rest. Looking back on it, I was so eager to go at that time, and the delay felt so long, but it was a fortunate thing because by the time I did go to the countryside, the Cultural Revolution was winding down, and the worst of the excesses were over.

In 1975 I graduated from high school (literally "senior middle school"). Those of us who had not yet gone out into the countryside were finally eligible to do so, and we had many discussions about it. The one I remember most happened two days after graduation, when I met my friends by the statue of Chairman Mao in Wangcheng Park. Naturally we were all thinking about what was going to happen next.

"I've heard that lots of *zhiqing* (urban youth sent down to the countryside) have never come back," said the boy we called Eyebrows due to his unusually bushy brows. "You could get stuck out there, doing physical labor for the rest of your life. No thanks!"

"You are so afraid of work, I don't know how you graduated," said Bai Jing, laughing at him. She was always teasing him.

"I do work!" he protested. "Just not at school, so you never see it."

"Don't you want to help make China great again?" Jianxiu asked him soberly.

"There are plenty of ways to do that," he said. "I have a good background, so why is digging in the dirt the only way I can help?"

"It is the most glorious way," I said. "You're talking bourgeois talk; you should be more careful."

"It's not bourgeois! Everybody can't work in fields and factories— someone has to run things."

"You just want to shoot guns," said Bai Jing.

"Jing is right," said Jianxiu, "you have to work harder if you want to join the PLA."

"That's where the real power is," Eyebrows said, puffing up his chest. "And there are other ways to get in."

"Well, I want to go to the countryside," I said. "Jin Xunhua is my hero, and I want to be just like him." My prized possession was a comic book of Jin's heroic life and death—one of the many ways the Party promoted him as an ideal revolutionary youth.

"You want to die?" Eyebrows laughed.

"If the village I get sent to has a river that floods, and the floods carry away two utility poles, I will be happy to die saving the people who retrieve the poles." I paused. "But I really don't think that is going to happen."

"To sacrifice yourself for the good of the country is a glorious way to die," Jianxiu said loftily.

"Does the greater power lie in the stick or the one who swings it?"

We all turned to gape at Bai Jing. Most of the time she was kind of silly, but once in a while she surprised us with her depth.

"I do not think he is going to be the next Chairman Mao," I said.

"The stick is the one that does the actual hurting," Eyebrows said defensively.

"Yes, but the one who swings it reaps the benefit," Jianxiu replied, obviously enjoying Jing's metaphor.

"Look, people are starving out in the countryside, and dying left and right of disease." Eyebrows looked scared now, his bravado gone. "I don't want to die. At least if I have a gun, I can defend myself."

"You two can follow Jin Xunhua off to Heilongjiang Province if you want, and freeze to death in the winter," said Bai Jing, eyeing me and Jianxiu. "I want to go to somewhere warmer." Changing the subject like this was one of the many ways we could tell that all her teasing of Eyebrows was just flirting—she did not like to see him suffer.

Jianxiu and I wanted nothing more than to follow in Jin's footsteps and finish the work he had started. First we had to apply to the central government of the city of Luoyang, where we lived. In our application, we told them we wanted to continue the work our hero had started. We spouted some popular Communist slogans, the best one being, "Criticize Lin, Criticize Confucius!" The fact that Lin Biao had died in 1971 and this was 1975 did not make the slogan any less meaningful, since it was used in several different ways until that year.

"Old Culture" was one of the Four Olds the Cultural Revolution was supposed to get rid of. The Communist Party believed that any part of traditional Chinese culture was bad because it came from the old feudal bourgeois society. And they especially targeted Confucius. So we intentionally quoted one of Confucius's teachings, "when your parents are alive, you should not travel afar," and then said, "This Confucius teaching can go to hell!"

And the city's central government actually approved us. But then they said we had to apply to the government of Heilongjiang Province. So we applied to them. We had to wait several months for a response, and when we finally received a letter from them, it said they had enough *zhiqing* in their province and that we should go wherever our school was going.

Jianxiu and I, however, were determined to prove that we were brave, tough revolutionary youths.

"We should not go to the same village," I said.

"I think we should get as far away from each other as we can," my friend agreed.

My eyes lit up at the idea. "We will deny ourselves even friendship."

"Yes!" She was getting excited too.

"And we will become great revolutionary heroes," I said.

"Even Chairman Mao will want to meet us and use us as examples for others to follow."

"We'll not see each other until Chairman Mao meets us in the Great Hall of the People."

"Deal!"

This was how we thought about everything. It was like the bumper sticker I see in America, "What would Jesus do?" except it was Mao. The fact that as far as we were told we would never return home, did not disturb our fervor.

When the day finally came, we were packed into a large truck, full of urban youths like me. There were twenty trucks in a convoy, and one of them was entirely filled with parents of the youths—including Mother. Each one of us had a big red paper flower pinned to our chest. In traditional Chinese paper cutting, red paper is commonly used to express good wishes, and these red paper flowers in particular were given to all *zhiqing* as they were sent off, as a symbol of honor and congratulations for the glorious thing we were doing. This was supposed to be a great patriotic undertaking. Of course we chanted slogans like "Educated youth must go to the countryside to receive re-education from the poor and lower-middle peasants!" and "Forging ahead courageously while following the great leader Chairman Mao" and "Be resolute, fear no sacrifice and surmount every difficulty to win victory."

The convoy traveled west up the Jian River valley with its terraced hillsides, then up into the hills and down into Sanmenxia in the Yellow River valley. The Sanmenxia Dam was a point of pride, built in 1956 and symbolizing China's glorious industrial future. Then we crossed into Shaanxi Province and followed the Wei River to Xi'an. Emperor Qin Shi Huang's collection of funerary statues, known in English as the Terracotta Army, had been discovered a few years earlier, but no one was interested in it because it was part of China's feudal past. Nor did it mean anything to us that Xi'an was the oldest of China's Four Great Ancient Capitals. We had been taught that there was nothing great in our past, only shame.

The trucks rolled south from there, across the Guanzhong Plain and up into the Qin Mountains. I had never seen mountains like this, not even from a distance. They rise sharply out of the plains to more than 10,000' in places, and help mark the dividing line between moist south China and arid north China. On the southern slopes, the vegetation is lush and home to pandas, monkeys, and many other animals—but we were to stay on the rugged, drier northern slopes. My truck swayed back and forth as it navigated the narrow, twisted road, and I felt sick to my stomach. Some of my classmates felt sick and threw up.

As the convoy rose up into the mountains, groups of us were dropped off in different villages. Many of the parents, especially the mothers, began to cry as they parted with their children. My classmates and I felt very sad too, but we wanted to show that we could be real revolutionaries, strong and tough, so we tried to control our tears. The hardest part was not saying goodbye to Mother, but parting from Jianxiu when the convoy arrived at her village.

We hugged so tightly. "I will see you again at the Great Hall of the People," I said. That was where we imagined Chairman Mao would meet us. She hopped down from the truck, and we watched each other as long as we could, while my truck continued up the road. My village turned out to be about thirteen miles from hers. That was as far away as we could get from each other.

When the truck reached the village I had been assigned to, my classmates and I got off the truck and stared, eager to see where we were going to be living. What we saw was a lot of dried mud—the villagers lived in plain, one floor, shabby cottages made from dried mud, which was all they had to build with. The hillsides surrounding us were mostly forested with a mix of pine, birch, oak, and larch trees, but it was a very rocky area and the mountaintops I could see were so craggy.

Our village, like the others we had passed through in the mountains, was very poor. It was late in the year, and a strong, chilly wind was blowing from the northwest. Of course the villagers did not have extra houses for us, so we had to stay with them at first, until they were able to build more houses for us. One of the few advantages of being poor was that rather than having to pay the government to build houses for us, they could just build the houses themselves out of mud. I and 24 other students from my school moved into the same house.

Most of the land was worked collectively and the peasants were not paid with money, or even food, but with "work points." Different kinds of labor paid a different amount of work points; men were paid more than women because they were considered more capable of physical labor. Poor rural communities like this were expected to improve their standard of living through self-reliance since the government could not afford to help them. What this really meant was that villages were at the mercy of their leaders' abilities. Dazhai Brigade was promoted as the model to study, because even though it was in a poor mountain area like ours, it managed to produce a lot of grain with its land, so the people had a good standard of living. But Dazhai's leadership group had been working together for several decades, so it was very effective (the fact that the government provided significant financial aid didn't hurt!). Our commune, production brigades, and production teams did not have such good leaders. When I arrived, even though the harvest had just been done, there was not enough food—and this happened almost every year.

There was very little good land, and not only did each team have to pay taxes and sell enough produce to the state to meet a quota, but it could only keep the profit from what was left over. Poor teams like ours were never able to produce enough to save up money for starting an industry that would have provided more income. The profit was divided between the members of the team based on each person's yearly accumulated work points. In some villages, a small percentage of the land was reserved for private plots in which individuals were allowed to grow whatever they wanted, and sell it to the state. But these villagers living in the mountains did not have that. Some people fainted from hunger.

Being sent up to the mountains or down to the countryside was not treated as a temporary change. The state controlled where each person lived, by issuing a certificate of residence to everyone. When *zhiqing* were sent to a rural village, their certificates were transferred to that village so that they were legal residents just like the inhabitants. That is why we could not just move back home when life in the countryside got difficult—although some people did. They used their *guanxi* (family connections) to get into a city and live illegally with relatives, or they just lived on the street. At that time the cities were so chaotic there were many gangs of people just living wherever they could and stealing what they needed.

Although our certificates of residence had been transferred here, we students did not receive the same food rations as we had in Luoyang. The government allotted us the same as each villager: received 50 kg of wheat, 300kg of corn, and 600kg of yams. We had to grind the grain ourselves to make flour. That was it for the whole year, and it was not enough. One time, I had been so hungry for so long that I started eating grass. It was a certain kind of grass that I had heard people ate in southern China, where they thought it was delicious. To me, it was just a way to survive.

Neither we nor the villagers had enough food. Life in the countryside was very poor and harsh with conditions which were unknown to us before. And while we had been trained to work in the fields, there were other basic skills like cooking that we did not have. At first we had a villager to cook for us, while later on we chose our own cooks. But we did not even know how to manage the food properly. The corn flour had a lot of bugs in it because no one had told us how to take care of it. During the day, when the sun was out, we could see the bugs and pick them out, but in the evening, or on dark winter days, we couldn't see the bugs, so we had to use the flour anyway. While we had wheat flour, we could make steamed bread to eat with lunch, and then we would have corn soup with each meal. But later on, after we ran out of wheat flour, all we had to eat was two steamed cornbreads. To work in the fields all day with that little to eat was so difficult for us, but that was how the peasants lived before we came—and after we left.

I wanted so badly to be a "model worker." At the end of the year, every production brigade would select someone whose work and behavior that year best represented the communist ideal. I worked so hard. I could do all the work the men did—plowing the fields, drying the wheat after harvest, collecting dung for fertilizer—and did not mind that I was given fewer work points than the men. And every year I was so proud to be selected as a model worker. The only reward for being chosen was a simple item like a shelf or a shovel. Just a shelf to put things on, or a personal shovel. It was a great honor, a serious reward, because they were expensive items that would be hard to get otherwise. Of course I did not need more than one of each, so I gave away the others. But I was more motivated by the idea that I was living up to the communist ideal, that I was a real revolutionary.

The difficulty we faced was more than hunger. More than ten of my schoolmates died during the three years I lived there. For instance, two male students in my village died when they were hit by trucks. And it was not an accident. There was tension between the local people and the urban youths. Like I said, the villagers were already poor and did not have enough to eat. And now thousands of youths had been sent to live with them and share the limited food. On their side, the youths were not used to going hungry, and some of them would steal fruit from orchards or vegetables from a garden or corn from the fields, or steal a chicken or even a dog—then cook it quickly and eat it. Big Nose stole some yams, and when the villagers tried to catch him, he fell down hill and died. Things like that gave all of us a bad reputation among the locals.

My village was about fifteen miles from the nearest market town. We urban youths did not have any form of transportation, not even bicycles, so to get to the town we had to walk. Though we could not move home, we were given leave to visit relatives, so we had to get to the town to buy a ticket to ride the bus home, which was a four or five hour drive. For some reason the male students especially did not want to walk that far, so they would try to hitch a ride with the local people. But because of our reputation, the locals didn't want to give a ride to these students, and two of them were run over in my village. The first one died just a few weeks after we arrived, and the second one was five months later.

Many *zhiqing* died from diseases. One of them was Jianxiu. Up in the mountains where we were, the only fertilizers we could use were natural ones, like mud from the river bottom and, of course, dung. My friend and I, since we wanted to be heroes like Jin Xunhua who was the first one to jump into the river, each of us was always the first one in our village to jump in to dig up mud, and the last one to stop. In early winter, the water was about knee-deep, so there wasn't much danger of drowning. We would dig up the silty mud at the bottom of the river and pull it out of the river onto a cart.

About a year after we arrived, at the beginning of the second winter, I received a letter from her. *Every afternoon lately*, she wrote, *I have had a fever. It is only a mild one, probably just a cold or something, but it makes working in the fields harder.*

You must be brave, I wrote back. *It is like the Party says, "Fighting on the battlefield does not stop for a minor injury."*

Since she wanted more than anything to be a brave revolutionary, Jianxiu didn't tell anyone how uncomfortable she was, and continued to work in the fields every day.

Several weeks later she wrote, *Today I returned home from the fields, and as I was walking up the hill to the village, blood started pouring out of my nose. I did not want anyone to see me, so I ran behind a bush. I lay down and pinched my nose and waited. Eventually the bleeding stopped. I went home and thought it was just a strange thing, but it happened again two days later.*

So I went to see the barefoot doctor and told her I wanted to learn about medicine so I could assist her. She was delighted, so I asked to borrow a book that would teach me to treat ailments of the head. I took the book home and read it immediately. It said to mash up some garlic and spread it on the soles of my feet. I did that, and my nose has not bled since then.

"Barefoot doctor" was the real term used for as many as a million young peasants with some general education who were trained to provide basic healthcare to their communities while they continued to work in the fields. They did often go barefoot.

I wrote to her how relieved I was, and how smart she had been to figure out the problem like that.

But later that week another letter arrived. *Now I have a rash, lots of tiny red spots all over my chest and belly. It started the day after I put the garlic on my feet, but I don't think it was the garlic. I'm frightened, Yee. Tan Ping* (another student in our class) *had a rash like this last year, and when she went home to see a doctor, the doctor told her she had leukemia. And she died several months later! Now I could have leukemia too. This is not a heroic way to die.*

Even the bravest soldier needs help with a serious injury, I wrote back to her. *Otherwise Norman Bethune would not have been able to help us against the Japanese during the War of Resistance* (the Second Sino-Japanese War). *You should go to your production team leader, show him the rash, and tell him what it could mean.*

So she went to her production team leader to show him the rash, and he gave her permission to go home to see a doctor. Her next letter did not arrive for several days, and I was so worried. I stopped right where I was when I received it, not bothering to sit down or anything.

I went straight to the doctor, before I even went home. He took some blood to run tests on it, so I had to wait several days. It was so hard. Mother got very upset with me because I did not feel like eating anything, I was so worried. Finally he called to say I should come back into his office. I ran the whole way there, which probably took longer, but I could not stand to wait for the buses. I burst into his office, ignoring the tea he offered me.

"What did the tests say?" I asked, panting. He must have thought me very rude.

"Your white blood cell counts are even higher than Tan Ping's. I am sorry, you have leukemia too."

I am so sad that I will not live to serve the Revolution. I will waste away and be forgotten.

I started to write Jianxiu a hasty letter to say I was going to visit her right away, then realized I would probably get there before the letter. So I ran to the head of my production team and begged for permission to visit her. Normally a visit to a friend for emotional reasons would not have been allowed, but I had proven myself such a model worker that I got special allowance.

The journey home felt so slow. I complained to myself, wondering why the Party did not build better roads out here, since these villagers were supposed to represent the bedrock citizens that everyone should learn from. I recited slogans and Mao quotations in my head, to try to encourage myself.

When the bus finally delivered me to Luoyang, I ran to Jianxiu's house. I found her surrounded by medical books and articles. She jumped up and ran to hug me so tightly.

"What does this really mean?" I asked.

"Here in China, most leukemia patients might live for up to a year, but in the West, people live five years and more."

For all the Party rhetoric about the West being decadent and inferior, China suddenly felt very backward. "Only a year?"

She nodded, then went to bring me tea. I looked more closely at all the books and papers; they were all about leukemia.

"It would be so easy just to distract yourself," I said as she returned with my tea. "But you are looking right at your disease."

"I do not want to be killed by a mystery," she replied. "If I die because someone shoots me, I see the gun, hear the shot, and feel it hit me. Maybe I find a hole in the wall behind me.

Maybe I find the casing. I can understand all those things. Why should this disease be different?"

"I guess it could be a lot worse than having a year to live," I said, trying to encourage her. "Imagine if you got run over by a truck like Xie Ning and Fan Shaoyun." But the words felt hollow even to me, and she did not seem to hear me.

"I might have gotten it from spending too much time in the river," she said. "The doctor told me that one of his patients was the County Governor of Huaibin, in the southern part of Henan."

"I hear there are a lot of rivers down there."

"Yes. The Huai River is the big one. The last time it flooded, the governor wanted to set a good example as leader, so he stayed behind after everyone else evacuated."

I could see where this was going. "He got leukemia?"

Jianxiu nodded. "He stayed in the floodwaters for three days, and found out later he had it."

It made me very sad to think that, by trying to demonstrate that she was a true revolutionary, my friend would lose her life to a disease. We had been willing to give our lives to further the revolution, but this didn't feel glorious. Chairman Mao had died several months earlier and the flames of our revolutionary fire had begun to die; Jianxiu's illness only dampened them more.

I felt some small measure of discomfort when some *zhiqing* in my village moved back to the city. For example, Jianxiu's leukemia diagnosis led me to find out that Western cancer patients lived longer and this caused an initial crack in my unwavering belief in the revolution. I wondered why anomalies like this could happen, and what future generations could learn from our experiences, from our passion, fanaticism, pride, tears and pains in the countryside. I began to have the first seeds of doubt about the rosy picture of socialist China painted by state propaganda.

CHAPTER THREE

I'm Leaving

One night early in the winter of 1977, Bai Jing came running into our house. I was two years into my time in the mountains, and Jianxiu had been home for a year. I felt grateful that she was still alive.

"The national entrance examinations have been restored!" Jing said excitedly.

"Did you hear that in town?" I asked. I knew she had gone with a group to the nearby market town.

"Yes! I guess Deng really means it when he says 'Respect knowledge, respect talent.' And you'll never guess what's different about it now."

"What?"

"There is no age requirement. You don't even have to have graduated from middle school!" (Remember, middle school included the American high school years.) Her eyes shone, and I could not believe what I had just heard.

"But we are stuck here—" I started, then clapped my hands over my mouth.

"What?" Jing stared at me, puzzled.

"I know the Cultural Revolution is officially over now [the announcement had been made in August], but I am so used to believing thoughts like that are counter-revolutionary, I can't help it."

"We *are* stuck here!" she laughed. "Everyone knows it."

"But now we have something to look forward to."

"Where are they going to find teachers? They have all been treated so badly. Who will want to teach now?"

"I hope this is a real policy change," I said wistfully. Policies had changed so radically so often during the Cultural Revolution, most people had become quite cynical about them.

I was fortunate. I passed the entrance examinations and left the village after only three years; the rest of my classmates went home the next year, but in some places *zhiqing* were already stuck in the countryside for years longer. In 1979, the government sent a committee from Beijing to visit *zhiqing* in Yunnan (which to us was a boring rural province). When the committee members gathered on a stage to give a speech to the youths, suddenly all the youths—thousands of them—knelt down on the ground, begging those leaders to ask the government to allow them to go home. Some had been there for ten years. That eventually led to the end of *zhiqin* movement.

China, along with other countries like South Korea, has a national entrance examination system for universities, called the National Higher Education Entrance Examination. It was created in 1952, but canceled at the start of the Cultural Revolution in 1966 and replaced with a new program that sent farmers, workers, and soldiers to college, though of course with a revised, politically-oriented curriculum.

There had been some signs of educational reform before 1977: withdrawing army representatives from middle schools in the early 1970s; reopening some universities in 1972—though with a politically-focused curriculum and a special student selection system; and then in spring of 1977, Deng's new slogans, "Respect knowledge, respect talent" and "All work, whether mental or manual, is labor."

Though Chairman Mao had died a year ago, and the Cultural Revolution was over, I had lived with revolutionary passion for so long that it only slowly waned. Especially a couple of years later, when some *zhiqing* left the countryside to move back and work in the city, Luoyang, according to some "rules" (many through family connections or feigned illness), one of them was a close friend of mine in our village, I began to feel somewhat depressed and couldn't see the hope of my future. Now knowing I could go back to school, though, certainly sped up its decline. I could not keep myself from looking forward to the end of my time in the countryside. So when the day came in 1978 that I was allowed to take the exams, I got permission to go back to Luoyang for study materials. No one really knew yet what it meant that the Cultural Revolution was over—we hoped for more social stability, and for an end to the political campaigns which changed direction so often that everyone had been burnt by them. But I knew I wanted to go back to school.

The day after I arrived in Luoyang, I heard a knock on the front door. I opened it to see a friend of mine standing there, panting.

"Miao Jianxiu wants to see you," she said before I could invite her inside. I hadn't had time to visit my best friend yet. "She's in the hospital." We did not have a phone, so she couldn't have called to tell us this.

"Did she say why she wants me?" I asked—not that I needed a reason to visit her, but I was curious what her urgency was.

"No, I'm sorry, that was all she said."

"Oh. Please come in."

"Thank you, but I have to get back. I just came to tell you that."

I thanked her, and we parted.

I went to see Jianxiu right away. When I walked into the hospital room, her parents were already there.

"I'm leaving," she said. I wanted so much to think she meant she was leaving the hospital because she was recovering, but the leukemia had been ravaging her body for almost two years. I knew what she meant.

"You've lived for much longer than a year," I said, hoping to encourage her.

"Please write a eulogy to read at my funeral." Her parents began to cry when they heard this.

I felt humbled that she would ask me. "Surely you would rather have someone else do that. I have never written one before."

"No one knows me as well as you do. I would rather have a simple but heartfelt eulogy than a clever but distant one."

"I will do my best." I squeezed her hand.

"Of course. Now please excuse me, but I want you to go home."

"I wish you wouldn't talk like this," said Mrs. Miao through her tears. "Maybe you will be one of the people who lives through this."

"Why are you begging her to leave?" Mr. Miao asked his daughter. "You asked to talk to your best friend and she came."

"I said what I wanted to say," Jianxiu replied. "I am tired. I am going to sleep now."

So I hugged her tearfully and left.

As I walked back outside into the sunshine, though my eyes squinted at the bright light and my skin felt the warmth, to me it was like darkness had descended over me. I couldn't see anything except darkness and the world felt like it was stuck in a long night. It was such a strange feeling. But I went home and wrote my eulogy, because she had asked me to.

I had been to funerals before, but it felt very different knowing I had to stand up and speak in front of the hundreds of people who had come. I read my tribute to my best friend, and I must have read it well—even though I was crying as I read it—because all the people listening started to cry as I read.

The death of my best friend, Miao Jianxiu, brought deep sadness to me. She was so smart, brave, hard-working, and always worked hard to be a true revolutionary, yet her life was stopped in her blooming youth after a brave journey with a disease. How sad it was to think of this, her life had just started, yet it was already over. These and other thoughts and questions churned in my head in those days. Though I could endure difficulties and suffering, such as strenuous work, scarce food, and isolation from cities in the countryside, my youthful hopes, illusions, and revolutionary belief began to dissipate. I subconsciously wanted to escape from settling for life as a peasant. I didn't want to be stuck in the bog, wasting my time day after day, and wanted to continue my interrupted education subliminally. Though without spelling it out to myself, I refused the life Mao and the Party had assigned to me.

Since there was no age requirement or limit, people as young as thirteen were among the millions who took the national entrance examinations which took two days that year (later took three days). During the first three years, only ten people from my high school graduating class were admitted to any university or associate professional school. The first year, less than 300,000—maybe 1%—were admitted nationwide, in part because some restrictions were set on admission: if you were married, your examination score had to be 100 points higher than unmarried applicants, and your *danwei* had to provide a letter of recommendation to confirm that you were a good person with a clean family history. In my case, I had to get a letter from my production brigade party leadership, and while I knew they would write that I was a good person, I didn't know for sure what they would say about my family background. During the Cultural Revolution, so much of the hardship and punishment that was inflicted on those with businesspeople in their family history was fickle and unpredictable; it depended on who happened to dislike you, or to envy you, or to decide avoid being targeted themselves by targeting you. So even though the Revolution had officially been over for two years, it took a while to believe that things had really changed.

The other major reason so few people were admitted was that for the previous ten years "intellectual" had been such a bad word, used to target and punish many teachers, professors, and scholars—and their family members. It was hard to turn all that around quickly. Also, academics were slow to trust that this pro-education attitude would last very long. As a result, there were too few schools and teachers to handle so many applicants. Because science and technology were one of the Four Modernizations announced in 1978 to push China toward becoming a great economic power, higher education was focused on practical knowledge that would advance China's industry and military. The humanities were not considered important.

I returned to the countryside, took the examinations, and passed. I was happy to find this way to leave the countryside, but sad that my friends could not leave with me; another year would pass before they were sent home. I was admitted to Henan University, which is in Kaifeng so I enjoyed getting to know the city my ancestors had lived in. I decided to major in English. It was, in part, a practical choice, because to achieve the Four Modernizations, China would need much more contact with the West and especially with America, so there would be a great need for English speakers.

Three Points, One Line. That was the slogan which described the life of university students in those early post-Cultural Revolution years. We went in a straight line between our dorm room, the dining hall, and the classroom/library. Okay, that is really four points, but only three activities. We had to eat and sleep in order to study, otherwise I think we would have done nothing but study. Everything else was considered a waste of time, and I really believed that. I studied so hard all the time. Those few of us who were admitted to university felt that our great fortune gave us a great responsibility. And I think the entire country felt like we had just lost ten years and had a lot to make up for.

I went even further than many students. I got up at 6 AM and went to sleep at midnight. I ate my meals after everybody else so I wouldn't have to waste time standing in lines. My first year I was chosen to join the university's basketball team, but I quit the next week because I thought the few hours I had to practice every afternoon were a waste of time. Studying was so competitive that if one person decided to get up at 5:30 AM instead of 6, many others would do the same.

In wintertime we were on the wrong side of the Yellow River. It has long been a major dividing line in China, and because we were south of the river, our building did not have a heating system—as though the cold air would stop when it came to the river. The school did provide our classroom with a stove in the back, but to keep the fire going for warmth, someone would have had to stop studying, and no one was willing to do that. So winters were very cold for us. My feet would be cold all night long.

My English literature professor caused me a lot of unhappiness, but not for anything related to my schoolwork. He was in his early fifties, he was single, and he felt affection for me which I did not return. He often invited me to lunch or dinner with him; I never went, even once.

One day after class, he handed me a book of poetry by a well-known Western poet.

"I'd like you to translate this into Chinese," he said. "I'll get it published, and put your name on it too."

I did not know what to say! It was so awkward, and I really did not want to do it. After a long pause, I said, "If you want to put my name on the book, please use a pen name."

"No, no! It has to be your real name so everyone knows you contributed."

I hesitated again. I was so nervous, afraid of upsetting the man who was teaching one of my favorite subjects. What would happen if he became angry? Would he grade me fairly after that?

"What's the matter?" he asked. "Don't you want credit for your work?"

"I haven't done any work. I am very sorry, it is so kind of you to make this offer, but I do not want my name on the book."

"No, it has to have both our names! It would be unfair of me to take all the credit for your work."

It was agonizing. Again I did not know what to do. The only way I could think to get out of the situation was to put off the decision. So I said, "Thank you for the book. I will read it and we can talk about it again next week."

His face lit up. "Thank *you!*"

That was a very difficult week for me. Why did he have to be so stubborn? I did not like that he was putting me in this situation, but I could not get out of it. I thought about it all week long, and had trouble focusing on my studies. On the seventh day, his class felt so long. All I was doing was waiting for it to finish so I could talk to him and get it over with. Then it felt even longer as the students left the classroom in no hurry.

"I looked through the book," I said as soon as the last student had gone. "It seems like very beautiful poetry, and I am afraid my English is not good enough. I would not be able to do justice to its elegance. I hope you can find someone else with better English."

It was another long agonizing moment. How would he take it?

He sat down heavily. "I wouldn't have asked you if I didn't think your English was good enough," he said sadly. "I'm sorry if I was mistaken." I think he finally understood that I was not interested in him.

He looked so disappointed. I genuinely felt sorry for him. But in my week of thinking, I had figured out what to do if he reacted badly to my decision.

"I am the one who is sorry. But after I graduate, if you have not married, you can live with me and I will treat you as though you were my real father." And I meant it. I had barely had a father, so it could have been a good thing for me.

Tears welled up in his eyes. "This poor old man does not deserve such kindness."

He did not take me up on my offer. When I graduated with honor in 1982, I was one of many English majors assigned to teach English. There was such a great need, and not just in Luoyang. Many of my classmates were sent to other cities, away from their families. But after all the struggle and pain of the Cultural Revolution—having to pretend to be ashamed of the scholars in my grandfather's family—I got to become a teacher just like he had been.

Teachers were expected to participate in meetings and political studies, but I had no interest in them, at all. And although most young teachers wanted to join the Party—for a variety of reasons, some idealistic and many practical—I had no interest in it. This caused me trouble with my

Figure 3.1. Color photograph of Henan University Entrance, which was built in 1935. From the Archives of the University History, Henan University.

Figure 3.2. Color photograph of Henan University former Library. This building was built in 1915. From the Archives of the University History, Henan University.

Figure 3.3. Color photograph of Henan University's former Research & Resource Center. From the Archives of the University History, Henan University.

department leaders. The school's Party Secretary said I was backward rather than progressive, and when I was eligible for promotion to the equivalent of Associate Professor, I was denied. If the president of the school had not intervened, I might never have been promoted.

While teaching there for eight years, I got married and had a son. In 1986, a number of major educational reforms were announced for higher education. The government would no longer control the departments, majors, and number of teachers in colleges and universities. Teachers were to be hired for two-to-four year contracts (rather than having a job for life, as was the case then) and chosen according to their academic level and teaching ability (rather than political fitness). Instead of receiving a stipend from the government, students who needed financial assistance for living expenses could receive scholarships and loans—provided they studied hard, obeyed the law, and followed discipline codes. Since the government assigned every graduate a job, the new employer would pay off the loan up front and receive reimbursement from the student's first five years of pay. Unfortunately, these reforms were implemented at some schools but not others, and not at mine.

In this atmosphere of expanding possibilities, Johns Hopkins University—one of the best universities in America—reached out to one of the best universities in China, Nanjing University, to establish a joint partnership. This became the Hopkins-Nanjing Center, and what caught my attention was that it had a graduate program in Chinese and American Studies. It did not offer a master's degree, only a one-year graduate Certificate, and accepted no more than 40 students from each country, but because American students would be studying there and American teachers would be teaching, the program offered a special opportunity to continue my studies in the United States. It would be much harder to do that from a Chinese university. The Center could give me connections to America that I would not have had, as well as a chance to adjust to dangle my legs in the waters of American culture without having to plunge in all at once.

Most importantly, though, it was an opportunity to study what I *wanted* to study—to choose a path for myself. Mastering English had been a means to an end—to get to the US—but obviously I was not going to teach English there.

So I applied, and it was a great honor to be accepted as one of those few students admitted from all of China in 1988. In keeping with the Center's mission to improve Chinese-American relations, the Chinese students studied with American professors, while the American students studied with Chinese professors and lived with a Chinese student as well. In every other Chinese school, foreign students not only lived in their own dormitories, but ate in their own cafeterias.

It was a very difficult adjustment for me. The American professors ran their classes just as they would at home, including a lot of reading. But although I was used to taking nine or ten classes each semester, Chinese classes tend to focus on taking notes in class in order to pass exams—in keeping with the traditional Chinese approach to learning. There is not much research or reading or paper writing outside of class, and now I had to do all that too. Reading and writing so much in a new language was also difficult and time-consuming. Although I had a young son now, I did not see him as much as I wanted to because I had to live at the Center, away from my family.

But I loved what I was learning, and wanted to study it more. I could not do that in China, so I decided I would try to go to school in America. It would be hard to do, for practical reasons. We could not afford for all of us to travel so far, and my husband was unable to get a travel visa at that time. So my family would not be able to go with me, at least not for some time, and I could not imagine living so far from them.

And there were yet more obstacles to face. During the Cultural Revolution, anyone who had gone to school in America was assumed to be a spy. Even twelve years after it ended, when I went home to Luoyang with my visa, it was still hard to find any information about American universities—even though Luoyang was a mid-sized city.

Furthermore, my salary at the time was only about 7 USD (54 RMB) per month which seems unimaginably small to Americans, but was much higher than most people's wages in China then because I had graduated from university. All wages were set by the government and they wanted to give people a good reason to go to university. Yet I was applying to American schools that wanted $25 just to submit an application. Applications to the four American schools would cost me fifteen months' salary. My good friend from the Hopkins-Nanjing Center, Ling gave me the information of the four American schools. Do the math for your own life, and imagine paying that much—not to go to college, but just for the *possibility* of going to college.

I also had to get a visa to enter the US. I wouldn't have been able to except that a journalist from the LA Times came to do an article on the Center, and happened to interview me and my American roommate Priscilla. Priscilla had come to the Center from Columbia University, where she got her bachelor's degree. So when I went to the US Embassy in Beijing to apply for the visa, I gave the visa officer the article to read, and even though it only included one quote from Priscilla, maybe the fact that she called me "a great roommate" made the difference, because he gave me the visa. Without that article, I might never have left China.

But even with the visa, I had mixed feelings. I was crying when I left the US Embassy. Part of me had hoped I would not get it. I felt it was so hard to leave my family, and especially my baby.

That summer right after his fifth birthday, my son had achieved his cognitive milestone. One early July day, he was suddenly awakened with apperception. That day, I brought him an art and science textbook for first graders and explained the first chapter to him. He was so interested in it and quickly learned the whole chapter with full comprehension. Then he requested to study the second chapter. After that, he insisted one more chapter and then another, although I suggested a few times that we should continue studying the following day. Eventually he finished learning the whole book within one day, which made me feel both happy and sad. I felt very sad and worried that I would miss playing a major role as a guide in fostering my son's development and learning. I was afraid that I would miss his first day of kindergarten or even his first day of school and miss helping him with his schoolwork since I didn't know how long it would be before I could see him again. This angst may have left me with sequelae that persists still to this day. In my dreams, my son was always around five years old, even last week. I've never dreamt about my son being older than five, not even once.

I also remembered another episode occurred early that year. That day in the middle of preparing Mother's birthday meals, I suddenly realized Mother was 60 years old, and I burst into tears. I thought Mother was only in her early fifties, how could she turn sixty so quickly? Sixty was quite senior to me at that time. How could I leave my old mother behind and travel ten thousand miles away to study in the US? I felt I was so unfilial.

The more I thought about this, the harder I cried. My husband tried to cheer me up by joking, "Okay, don't cry. We just tell them we don't want to go!" And it was true, I did not want to go. But I also wanted to go. If I stayed, I could see what my life would be like in 20 or 30 years from the example of the senior faculty in my department: a plain, bored, and dissatisfied life without much of a chance to improve my English. First, my school was not a target university in the country, meaning that I wouldn't be eligible for the very few scholarships from Western universities at the time. Second, the candidates for these rare scholarships were all been chosen by the authorities, and party membership was a prerequisite. I had no chance, for not only being a non party member, but also for being criticized as politically backwards by the department head even if my school had a chance at one of these scholarships. So, if I stayed, I would only gradually lose what I had learned from school since there was no environment to speak the language outside my classes. On top of that, I had to sit through endless, tedious meetings twice a week.

A thought first occurred to me while I was an undergraduate student and selected as one of the two interpreters for foreign guests who came to visit our university: how wonderful it would be to go and study in the West! I remembered how I was shocked with admiration when hearing one couple saying that they were going to spend their Christmas vacation in Hawaii. Hawaii was paradise to me. This freedom and the capability to see Hawaii, something that I could only dream of, tormented me.

Then another friend of mine told me her story in the US. She was sent to the US to study for two weeks and was allowed to stay one night at her American friend's home. She was excited to find out that the couple had four bedrooms. They told her that she could sleep in a different bedroom each night if she wanted. I could not fathom how two people could own a house with four bedrooms!

Then I heard more stories of America, a land of freedom and opportunity. I dreamt about going to America to study someday. This dream always remained firmly rooted in my mind. In the end, following my dream of studying in America was the stronger feeling and overcame all other resistance.

Three of the schools accepted me, and I decided to go to Indiana University of Pennsylvania because I had two friends already living in Pennsylvania. I was going to leave my family, my friends, my home, and my country, to go to a place that I had grown up believing was the enemy.

It seemed to me that the whole town had made its way to the train station on the day of my departure. A large group of friends had gathered to bid me farewell. I was one of the first to go to the West from our quiet town, and the thought of such a long journey, with the prospect of living among a strange and possibly hostile people so far away from home had hushed my friends into an awed silence. When the train whistled its signal for departure, all my friends and I burst into tears as I waved them goodbye from the window.

CHAPTER FOUR

The Little Match-Seller

I had traveled several hundred miles from home to go to the Hopkins-Nanking Center, but I had never flown on an airplane before. The distance from Luoyang to Pennsylvania was more than I could imagine. It was a long series of flights, and I was terribly airsick most of the way. I was so relieved when we landed in New York—assuming the airsickness would go away. But it did not.

Priscilla's sister picked up me at the airport and took me to their parents' house, which was across the street from Columbia University. I still felt sick. Here I was, finally in America, in New York City no less, and I could not enjoy it. Hearing about it from Priscilla and other American students at the Hopkins-Nanking Center, I had imagined many times what it would be like. I could never have imagined that instead I would feel so sick for so long, unable to do anything but lie in bed. I wanted to walk around just looking at this big city that so many people talked about like it was the center of the world.

I stayed the night, then flew to Pittsburgh still sick. That airplane was the smallest one I had been on. It felt cramped, and it bounced around in the air much more than the other airplanes had, so I had the most terrible airsickness. I felt so nauseous and dizzy, and threw up multiple times throughout the flight. I was still feeling horrible when I landed. Then I had to take a bus and a taxi to get to Indiana. Despite how unfamiliar everything was, and how inadequate my English felt, I would probably have been excited, but I could not enjoy the hills, the fields, or the forests we passed, and I still felt horrible when I arrived at IUP.

Three days passed, and nothing changed. Looking back at it, I think it might not have all been airsickness. I was overwhelmed by the strangeness of everything around me, afraid, and homesick. Then—this was very confusing—I began to feel hungry even in the midst of my sickness.

As I walked across campus that night—pulling my thin jacket closed against the breeze that was so much colder than Luoyang in late summer—I ran into a student from Taiwan who I had met the day before.

Although Taiwan is south of China, the official language is Mandarin, so we were able to talk fairly easily—certainly more so than if we had used English.

"You look awful," he said.

"I feel awful."

"You're still sick?"

I nodded. "It's so strange, though. This morning I started feeling hungry too, at the same time that I feel sick."

"Maybe that's a good thing. It's normal to feel hungry when you haven't eaten for so long."

"Then why do I still feel sick?"

He shrugged. "Try eating something."

"The cafeteria's closed."

"So go to a restaurant."

"I can't afford it."

"Can you afford to spend a dollar?"

I did not expect that question! "Maybe. That depends on what I'd get for it."

"There's a place, Joe's Hot Dogs, where you can get two hot dogs for a dollar. Have you ever had a hot dog?"

I shook my head.

"It's very American. A tube of spiced, ground pork meat inside a bun, with sauces like ketchup and mustard. You should try it!"

My stomach growled at the thought of eating. "Thank you, I will."

I followed the directions he gave me, and went into the restaurant. It was more of a fast-food place, and while American chains like McDonald's and Kentucky Fried Chicken had spread to China in the 1980s, I had never been inside one. So it was a strange experience, and I had some trouble just reading the menu and figuring out how to order. But I spent the dollar, got my hot dogs, and went to a little table to eat them. I took a bite, and my first impression was that the meat tasted good. Then I swallowed, and my stomach was so unhappy. I took one more bite—and ran for the bathroom to throw up.

Looking back now, I am not surprised I was unable to eat it—it was so different from anything I had eaten before, and my stomach was already so unhappy I probably could not even have eaten rice. But there was very little I could afford at that point, since I did not yet have a job, so I felt that saving money was the most important thing. That was the first American food I ate, and to this day I cannot stand hot dogs.

There are many differences between the US and China that I imagine are obvious, such as the food (and even that difference is greater than you would think, because few of the meals sold in Chinese restaurants here are real Chinese food), the language, the architecture, social conventions, and so on. There are also differences that would never have occurred to me, such as the smell of sweat. I arrived in the US in late summer, and the first time I found myself in a crowd of Americans, I was amazed to discover that they smelled different. I can only assume it has something to do with the difference in diet, but the smell of their sweat distinctly differed from what I was used to among Chinese. That, perhaps more than anything, made me feel like I was among a strange people.

At that time, international students were allowed to work no more than twenty hours a week on campus. I think the idea was that it would be good for us to get out into the community, to expand our horizons as the phrase goes. So I worked in the cafeteria for twenty hours a week, and since that first year I did not have a scholarship, my income had to pay for everything—including the textbooks, which were very expensive for me. Even at minimum wage, I was making as much money per hour as I had made per *month* in China, but of course everything costs more here too. Most students who came from mainland China back then were poor. Over the course of the first year I only remember spending one dollar to buy ten clothes hangers to dry my clothes on after I washed them, and a little money here or there for some food that was on sale, like celery, carrots, maybe pork or chicken.

We Chinese students had to work so much harder than the American students. Even though I had graduated from the Johns Hopkins program in Nanking and lived with Priscilla for a year, in my first semester at IUP I could understand less than half of the lectures. Understanding some of the professors was even harder because they had accents. I would guess my American classmates might have needed two hours for the readings for one class, but it would take me four to six hours—sometimes more— for the same readings because I had to look up so many words. I lugged my English-Chinese dictionary with me everywhere, in addition to my textbooks and notes. And there was so much reading! Even with my experience at the Hopkins-Nanking Center, being taught by American professors, I was not prepared for how much reading we had to do. The schoolwork took so much time that I often got only a few hours of sleep.

So life was really hard at that time. I was terribly homesick. I missed my son, my husband, my mother, and everything familiar and comforting. For the first three months I think there were tears in my eyes constantly. My loneliness was profound. I remember one winter night, I was lying on my bed, looking out through the window at the heavy snow falling. The snowflakes were drifting down from the sky, floating in the air, and when they passed through the streetlight they seemed to grow. What were my family members doing, I wondered—especially my baby, who was still with my husband in China. Across the Pacific Ocean there were thirteen hours time difference between the two countries. Were they all thinking of me this moment? Were they missing me too? Tears ran down my cheeks.

Because money was so scarce, I realized I needed a cheaper place to live. During Christmas break, on another snowy night, a friend took me out to look for a cheaper apartment. She turned the car's heater up because I did not have much warm clothing. We drove carefully around the area near campus, with a newspaper to guide us but also hoping to come across "room for rent" signs. I really needed to be able to walk from home to campus, since paying to take the bus would have cost money I could not afford. The gently falling snow, and the lights shining from the houses, made the houses look beautiful. But the sight just made me sad.

"It looks so nice and warm in all these houses," I said. "How can there be so many houses and no rooms for me?"

"I'm sure we'll find one," she said with a cheerful smile. "University towns like this have to have plenty of cheap housing. College students never have much money."

But all I could think of in that moment was "The Little Match-Seller" by Hans Christian Andersen, a short story about a young orphan girl, all alone on the street on a snowy night, trying to make a living selling matches. As she huddles against the cold, she lights her matches for what little warmth they bring—and begins to imagine things in the match-flames: a warm fire, a Christmas tree, a tasty goose to eat, and her dear departed grandmother. As glorious as those visions seemed to her, in reality she was freezing to death.

I did find a cheaper apartment on Philadelphia Street, one of many rooms in a building with four or five floors. Most of the renters were other students from China, and it was much cheaper than the other apartments I had looked at. The first day, when I moved in, I saw roaches running all over the floor. So many roaches, dead and alive. I stayed there for twelve nights, and it was so hard to sleep knowing roaches were everywhere. Then I moved out.

I finally found a place to settle for the next year, renting a room from an older woman who went by the name Beef, which was a nickname for Elizabeth. She was nurse in WWII. She had married a southerner, who was a pilot in WWII. Yet her in-laws never accepted her because she was a Yankee. Then, while she was pregnant with her third child, her husband died. When I met her, she had been single ever since—for four decades—and her children had all moved away.

The "study-eat-sleep" triangle we had joked about at Henan University was still with me during the first year and a half of my master's program. I was just trying to get by until my family could join me.

Chapter Five

Poison Ivy

I had arrived at IUP in late August, 1991 and lived there by myself, on the other side of the world from my family, for a year and a half. It took that long for my husband to put together enough money to afford the airplane fare for him and our son. Finally the day came in March, 1993 when they arrived. It was cold and sunny, and there was still snow on the ground from the blizzard the week before—the "1993 Storm of the Century." I did not have a car, but a friend drove me to the airport in Pittsburgh, which was the nearest city. We got there early because I did not want to miss my family if the flight was early, but that meant we had to wait longer. It was so hard to wait for my family to walk off the airplane. I strained to see past the people streaming out of the gate, desperate for a glimpse—and there they were at last. Although he was clearly exhausted, my husband ran to me, pulling my son behind him. I started to cry as I hugged the man I had not seen for so long. We did not say anything because no words seemed adequate. Then I kneeled to greet my six year old son, Chris. I could not believe how much he had grown while we were apart. He clung to my husband, seeming to feel shy, as though he wasn't sure who I was.

"Chris, you must remember me—I'm your mama! I am so sorry I had to be here without you."

He looked at me, still seeming to feel shy.

"Come hug me! I have missed you more than you could ever guess."

It took more urging, but he did hug me at last. As hard as it had been to be apart from him for so long, it had never occurred to me that he would feel distant from me. At his age, a year and a half must have seemed like an eternity.

Together we went to live in the upper floor of a large garage some distance from campus. It was so much more living space than we ever had in China, and it felt strange to have so much space for so little stuff. Since we had two bedrooms and were living in America now, we thought we should use both rooms, so we gave my son his own room. That first night, in the middle of the night, Chris woke us up as he came running into our room, crying. I was worried, of course, but I also felt relieved when he jumped into my arms—all his shyness forgotten.

"Chris, what's wrong?" I asked.

"I'm scared."

"What happened? Did you have a bad dream?"

He nodded as I wiped away his tears.

"You're safe with us now." I pulled him into the middle, between us. We listened as he told us about his dream, which was something involving demons from the Chinese classic *The Journey to the West*.

"Why do I have to sleep in the other room?" he asked when he finished.

"Maybe you don't," said my husband. "We thought we'd try it that way because that is how Americans live."

"Stay here with us tonight," I said. "Tomorrow we'll figure out what makes sense."

The next day we decided that it made more sense to sleep together in one room. That was what we were used to.

We had our own phone line in the apartment, which felt like a luxury. We didn't use it to call anybody, but since my husband's business involved people in China, we let them call us—until we got the bill for the first month. We could not believe how much money those international calls cost, so we never used the phone again.

When my son first arrived in America, I was worried about how thin he was, especially compared to other American children his age. I suppose that he had not had the same advantage of growing up with beef injected with growth hormones, and traditional Chinese food usually entailed a more moderate calorie count. In order to get him to grow, we encouraged him to try out for various sports teams at school. He tried baseball, but ended up running cross country and playing lacrosse in Middle and High School. He ended up being pretty good at lacrosse, though he was always at a significant disadvantage versus some of the boys his age who were significantly bulkier in size. He even continued playing through the first year of college at the local lacrosse club.

Of course we tried to help Chris get bigger by feeding him American food. McDonald's was the first idea that came to mind, but we were so short on cash at the time! Chris still remembers my husband and I taking part-time jobs cleaning houses for $50. When we got back, we would always have bought him some American fast food which he happily devoured after practice. Chris is much taller, bigger and stronger today. We still believe it had much to do with the McDonald's we fed him all those years ago.

My husband went through a period of horrible luck. The house we lived in had a huge yard that needed a lot of work to maintain. During the summer and fall, my husband helped out by mowing the lawn, refusing payment every time because we were so grateful to live there. One day he came to me as I was studying. I looked up, and saw that he had some redness on his face and arms.

"I have some kind of rash," he said. "It itches like crazy."

"If you don't know what it is, you probably shouldn't scratch it."

"Easy for you to say!"

Since neither of us knew what it was, I didn't think much of it at that point, though that night I found out it was on parts of his chest too. But every day it got worse, and he couldn't help scratching sometimes. The skin got red and developed blisters, and the swelling continued. A week later, his face was so swollen he could not open his eyes. All the affected areas now hurt as well as itching horribly. We did not know what was wrong, and we did not have health insurance so we could not afford to see a doctor. We were so worried. Finally the wife of the couple we were renting from saw him, and she said it was poison ivy. We had never heard of poison ivy—although there is a lacquer tree in China that I have heard has a similar effect—but she said sometimes it grew on the edge of their yard.

Money continued to be a real struggle. At the beginning of my second year I received a scholarship, but now there were three of us, and my husband could not work legally at first. In addition to my twenty hours a week in the cafeteria, I started working several hours a night in a Chinese restaurant. Minimum wage was over $6/hour, but the restaurant paid me much less than that because I supposed to get tips. However, I had never got even $1 tips in life because I was only at the rank of a busboy/busgirl.

Our first car was a very old one which was given to us for free by our good friends Ed and Becca. My husband wanted to change the oil himself, because he said it was easy and would save us money. That made sense to me, so he got his tools and went to work.

Not much time passed before he came running to me, a bloody rag wrapped around his left hand and a pained look on his face.

"I cut my hand," he said.

"What? How did you cut your hand changing the oil on a car?"

"One of the parts was really hard to get off," he said. "I had to put all my weight on the wrench, and when it finally gave way, I fell on a sharp edge."

He pulled the rag off to show me—it was such a long, deep cut, very painful and bloody.

I had to look away. "What are we going to do? We can't afford to see a doctor."

It would never have occurred to us to do what so many Americans do: go to the emergency room at a hospital and worry about paying for it later, even if that meant being in debt.

"I am a doctor, you know." It was true, he had graduated from medical school and worked as a doctor for ten years in China.

"I do know, but how can you do anything when you only have one hand?"

"You could help me."

I shook my head. "I can't bear to look at it."

He got a little frustrated then. "I have to do something! The wound could get infected, or my hand could heal badly so I can't use it. I am going to the store."

He wrapped up his hand again, and went off. Half an hour later he came back with rubbing alcohol, hydrogen peroxide, tape, and other first aid stuff. He went into the bathroom and closed the door while I waited anxiously outside. At one point I opened the door a crack and peeked through—and almost fainted. There was so much blood, and one of his bones was exposed. I don't know how he could do it, but he did, and he must have done a good job because he did not get an infection. To this day he has a long scar across his left hand.

We had trouble of a different kind with our second car. I was on my way to school, waiting in an intersection at a red light. Another car approached from the side, and stopped like it should, but suddenly went forward again and crashed right into me. It knocked me almost 360° around. I was so dizzy, though not hurt. I stayed in the car until a police officer came. She talked to me, and talked to the other driver, and then she gave me a ticket. I did not understand why.

Another driver had witnessed the crash, so I walked slowly over to talk to him. He actually looked a bit familiar.

"You saw what happened, didn't you?" I asked him.

"Yeah—did the cop really give you a ticket?"

I nodded.

He shook his head. "It wasn't your fault at all. Hey, are you a college student?"

I nodded again.

"I thought so. I give lectures there every week."

I would have smiled, but I still felt dizzy. "I think I have seen you before."

"Anyway, I'm an officer in the Air Force, and I'd like to write you a letter stating what I saw and making it clear you were not at fault. That ought to help you clear this up."

Now I could not help but smile. "That is very kind, thank you." I gave him my address and went off to catch the bus to school.

Four or five days passed before I received his letter. When I went to the insurance office to show them the letter, they said they had already paid the other driver's claim. I did not have any experience with the US legal system, but I did not want anyone to think I had caused the accident, or to have to pay more for my insurance, so a friend referred me to a lawyer. We did wind up going to court to prove my innocence, and the judge said the crash was not my fault. Unfortunately, even with that result from the court, my insurance company still said it was too late, there was nothing they could do.

In the spring of 1993, I finished my master's degree and applied to doctoral programs. My first choice was Carnegie Mellon, partly because Pittsburgh was not very far away and I could easily visit my friends in Indiana, PA. I drove to the campus twice for interviews. The Chinese history professor there took a liking to me and really wanted me to be his student with him as advisor. But when the department's decision finally arrived in the mail, it was a rejection. The reason they gave was that they only had one Chinese history professor and his area of expertise differed too much from what I wanted to study. They did not think he could be an effective advisor to me.

This explanation did not make sense to me, but I think there was another thing that might have affected their decision. There had been a conflict between a different professor and a student of his in the history department. Since that professor was the only one in his field, they could not just assign the student to a different advisor as they would normally do. The department had a hard time deciding what to do with the student; finally they let him go to University of Pittsburgh to take more classes. So they were afraid something similar would happen if they accepted me, but that reason made even less sense to me.

In the end, I wound up at the Ohio State University.

Chapter Six

A Drop of Blood

Dr. Rife helped us move to Columbus, Ohio. He was my teacher, a good friend, and a father figure to me by now. He rented a mid-sized U-Haul truck, but we did not have much to put into it: two mattresses, a computer table, our old computer, a couple chairs, a few pots and pans, plates and bowls and utensils, and our meager clothing. He helped us unload the truck into our new apartment—which didn't take long. When he was done, and I realized he was leaving, I burst into tears. I had put off facing the fact that we were starting all over again, and now I felt so sad, like an abandoned baby.

We only owned used stuff. We bought some cheap furniture from yard sales, and found a lot of it free on the side of the street, even next to someone's garbage. At the end of each semester, we would drive around campus and the area nearby looking through the stuff the graduating students were getting rid of. Once again, it was such a strange phenomenon from a Chinese point of view. During the Cultural Revolution, consumer items like TVs, radios, and bicycles were not a priority, so few were manufactured. You had to have a government-issued coupon even to have the option to get one, and even then there might not be enough available in your area. The situation improved during the 1980s as production of consumer items increased, but there was still enough sense of scarcity that the idea of something like a yard sale would never have occurred to anyone. There was also a cultural difference: Chinese were much more likely to give the occasional extra item to a friend or family member.

We had found a $300/month apartment to rent, in a building full of other international students who were also drawn by the cheap apartments. At that time Chris, who was seven, did not have many toys. One weekend we came across a yard sale, and I found a Nintendo game system. It was only $8, so I bought it. Chris was so happy. It was his first real toy, and he played it a lot on our little TV.

After the first quarter of school, I realized we did not have enough money to pay the tuition for the next quarter. So we decided that I would quit school for a couple quarters or a year, so I could work to earn enough money to pay for it. But I didn't want to have to reapply. I asked around, and found out that it was possible to get a kind of suspension for medical reasons, that gave you time off to get better and then pick up where you left off. So we came up with a plan.

I took my husband with me to the student clinic at the university. This was my first experience with an American health care system, and I did not know what to expect. Getting to see an actual doctor took much longer than I was used to. First I had to explain to the receptionist why I was there.

"I think something is wrong with my kidneys," I said.

"What makes you think that?" she asked.

"I have really bad back pain and I am not making much urine."

Then I had to wait for a nurse. Then I had to explain it again to a nurse. She, at least, checked my vital signs, but then I had to wait again. I began to wonder how many times I would have to repeat myself, and although the doctor was the next person to come into the room, I still had to tell him all over again. *Do they not talk to each other?* I wondered. He felt all over my stomach and my back, and listened to them with his stethoscope.

"Everything sounds okay," he said.

I wondered what kidney disease was supposed to sound like; I could not fake that.

"Do you take pain medicine on a regular basis?" he asked.

I shook my head.

"And you've never had cancer or lupus or been treated for them."

I nodded.

"How's your diet? Do you each much meat or dairy?"

"No." He probably thought that was some virtuous choice on my part, but of course it really had to do with money.

"Well," he said, "There are quite a number of possible causes of kidney disease, assuming that's what we're dealing with. Abdominal pain can be very difficult to trace because the area you feel the pain may not be anywhere near the source of the pain. But low urine output does suggest a kidney problem, so we'll start eliminating the causes that are easier to identify. We'll need blood and urine samples."

Then he left, and we waited again. Eventually the nurse returned with several kits. She filled two vials with my blood, then handed me a urine test kit and explained how to use it.

"I'll come back in ten minutes," she said. "Take your time." And she walked out.

I looked at my husband. "Ready?"

He nodded.

We walked out of the room and into the hallway, then followed the nurse's directions to the bathroom. We looked around, and waited a minute or so until no one else was around. Then I went into the bathroom—and my husband hurried in after me.

I followed the instructions for the urine kit. When I had filled the little plastic bottle, my husband took a cloth out of his pocket, unfolded it, and picked a needle out of the cloth. He carefully pricked one of his fingers with the needle, and when a drop of blood formed, he let it fall into my urine sample. I screwed the cap on tightly, then shook the bottle to mix in the blood while he washed his finger and waited for it to clot.

We had to be very careful at that point, since it is easier to sneak into a room than to sneak out. We decided that he should go first, since it should look like he had never left the room. I was so nervous, and my husband reassured me, but I had to wait several minutes after he left, before leaving the bathroom myself—and those minutes were hard. I did not know if anyone had seen him, or if he had been caught. But when I stepped out into the hallway, everything seemed normal. I walked back to the examination room, and he smiled at me from a chair. We had gotten away with it.

When the urine test result came back, it showed that I had a form of kidney disease, so I was allowed to quit school for the semester. The doctor was puzzled because I did not have any of the other symptoms of that form of kidney disease, but he did not question it. He said there are always a few people whose diseases act differently. In China people often resorted to tricks like this to get around the stifling bureaucracy, but here it felt different. I did not like having to do it. It made me feel even worse about the poverty that had driven us to such lengths.

Chris was always a bit of a late bloomer. When we first moved to Columbus, I was a little worried about Chris's development as the other boys his age at school seemed to be more mature and clever. However, Chris quickly became fluent in English through the ESL (English as a Second Language) classes. He worked hard and his grades were good by the end of the first year.

Chris has always been rebellious in nature. In Middle School this rebellious streak began to appear, much to our surprise given the authoritarian upbringing we ourselves had. Chris always aimed to improve his social standing and starting hanging out with the cool kids.

In college he even started getting into physical fights, mostly in defense of the fraternity he had joined. He even started an informal mixed martial arts club during his time at the University of Chicago. Despite the monumental task of learning to fit in as an immigrant from the opposite side of the world without much help from us, he still maintained good grades. He was accepted in the Kentucky Governor's Scholars Program his junior year in High School, which was a program designed to keep the top performing students from leaving Kentucky after they graduated. Chris ended up leaving Kentucky anyway for first Chicago and then New York City.

We did not know this could happen, but eventually Chris played his Nintendo so much that his vision got worse—so bad that he needed glasses. We kept putting it off because glasses are so expensive, but not being able to see started to affect his schoolwork. He moved up to the second row in class, and then to the front row, and then the day came he still could not see the blackboard. So we had to spend the money.

We walked into the eye doctor's office, and even though we could see the walls of glasses on display, we went straight to the front desk.

"My son needs glasses," I said. "What are the cheapest frames and lenses?"

"That depends," the receptionist said, "on how big the frames need to be and how strong his prescription is. We have to do some measurements first."

"At school he cannot see the blackboard from the first row. Can you give us any kind of estimate?"

She hesitated. "Well, our cheapest frames start at $115, and the lenses. . . ." She consulted a chart. "They might be around $50 to $70 if you don't get any extra features."

My husband and I looked at each other. That was so much money to us.

I think she figured out what we were thinking. "If money is an issue, you might qualify for a low income discount."

"How do we get that?"

She reached into a drawer, pulled out a piece of paper, and handed it to us on a clipboard with a pen. "Fill out this form."

We took it back to a chair to look at. It was full of questions about money—our income, how much money we spent on food every month, that sort of thing. The receptionist had assumed we knew how this kind of discount worked, but we did not.

I put down $150 for our monthly food expense.

"That is too much!" my husband objected. "We don't spend anywhere near that much."

"I know, but we want to seem normal." In those days I worried a lot about fitting in. Of course, putting down a higher expense would give us a better chance of getting the discount, but we just did not think like that. In China most jobs were provided by the government, so you could not get away with lying about your income.

I finished filling out the form and handed it back. The receptionist scanned through it, and when she came to the food expense question, she looked up.

"I'm sorry, I think you made a mistake on this question."

She handed me the clipboard and pointed to the question.

"No, that is correct," I said.

"Oh my God, that's unbelievable. How can you only spend $150 on food per month?"

I did not know what to say. What would she think if I told her we only spent $80 a month on food? Her reaction made it clear that I had no idea what normal was for Americans. In the end, though, it would not have mattered how I answered that question; since we did not have green cards, the doctor could not give us a discount.

We became friends with another Chinese family, the Nis. Like us, they did not make a lot of money, but they tried really hard to save. They shared a two-bedroom apartment with another family, and the apartment was half underground so it was even cheaper. None of us used much air conditioning or heating, but they didn't use any heat at all in winter. Maybe the fact that they were living partly underground made that easier, but Columbus was very cold in winter.

Since they all lived together, we became friends with their roommates too, the Jia family. They had a son who was a few months older than Chris. They played together and the kid often came to our house. After a long weekend trip to visit friends in Indiana, PA, we got home at midnight. We opened the door to our apartment—and I will never forget what I saw.

Everything was turned over and scattered on the floor. I was shocked. I thought we had been robbed. Although we didn't own anything expensive at all, it was frightening all the same. We picked our way around, looking at the mess and wondering why anyone would want to rob us. Eventually we recovered enough to think of calling the police. While we waited for them to come, we started to clean up and put things back where they belonged.

That was when we figured out who had done it. The first clue came from some Chinese paper and brush pens I had brought from China to keep up my Chinese writing; written on one piece of paper were the characters for the Jia kid's name. Then we discovered an empty soft drink can; we had bought some soft drinks for Chris recently because they were on sale. We also realized that someone had taken our whole collection of quarters, which we used at the laundromat. The last clue was that one of the keys to the apartment door was missing. So it was clear that the Jia kid had stolen the key one time when he was visiting us, and had used it to get in while we were away. At that point there was a knock at the door.

"I hope that's the police," said my husband as he went to open the door.

And it was—a pair of police officers. "You reported a break-in?" one of them asked.

"It was just a little kid," said my husband.

"He stole a key from us," I explained, "and used it to get in while we were gone. But all he took were some quarters."

They looked around at the mess, and I could tell they were not sure whether to believe us. "So you know who did this?"

I nodded. "It was our friends' son."

"Do you want to press charges?"

My husband and I exchanged glances. We each knew what the other was thinking. He was just a little kid, so young. We did not want to give him a criminal record for this.

"No," I said. "It's okay. We will work it out with his parents."

Then it was the police officers' turn to exchange glances. "You're sure?"

"Yes." I was beginning to feel nervous that maybe they would not believe us.

"Okay. Hope you folks have a better day."

And they left. We called the Jias right away and told them that they needed to teach their son to behave properly.

My husband worked very hard at his business during these years. He went through countless difficulties and setbacks, but never gave in, never stopped trying. For a while, most of his income came from a big order once a year that brought him $10,000 in profit. Obviously that is not much income from a whole year. We got a break at the beginning of my second year, when I was granted a scholarship that many Ph.D. students got, of $900 per month through the end of the seven year program. I also began to work as a Teaching Assistant and a Resident Advisor. After several years I was allowed to teach Asian civilization classes.

Those things helped us financially, but as Chris grew it became more expensive to feed and clothe him. I remember my husband and I would be out driving somewhere, and as we passed different restaurants we would say, "When we have money, we'll eat there," and we'd laugh and imagine what it would be like to eat that delicious food. But aside from those rare moments of laughter, I felt there was no hope for the future, and this poor academic life felt endless. Life continued to be really hard.

One time I went with my husband on a business trip to visit a potential customer. We drove back through Pennsylvania, through mid-state New York, and into southwestern Connecticut. I had been to New York City once or twice, but never to Connecticut. We marveled at all the enormous houses, like mansions dotting the land. Just before we got to the man's office, I changed into the black "power suit" I had bought for job interviews—and maybe it helped, because we made a deal with him. But still there was a problem. We had student visas, but we did not have green cards, and our visas only allowed us to enter the US twice in a six month period. If you wanted to enter a third time during that period, you had to go to the US embassy in the country you were visiting, to get a new visa—which was risky in China because visas were very difficult to get. I did not go home at all for the first six years after arriving at IUP.

So when we got our first order from the new Connecticut customer, we were unable to go back to China to supervise the manufacturing (it was a special metal for a Boeing plant). And they made a mistake. It was a minor mistake, less than one tenth of a percent off, but it was enough to ruin the order, and we lost the customer.

I went back to China for the first time in 1997, and took Chris with me. I wanted to visit friends and family, of course, but I also needed to conduct research for my dissertation. Despite the fact that I was not a businessperson, my husband thought my being there was an opportunity to visit a potential customer, so he asked me to go to southern China to sign a contract with a supplier. I left Chris in Luoyang with Mother and took an overnight train that went through the Qin Mountains. The moon was bright enough that I could see the tree-covered mountains as we passed through them. Occasionally we would pass a few lights and I would imagine what those people's life was like. I wanted to imagine it as a romantic, mysterious life, but I believe in reality it must be very hard; I do not think much had changed for them since I lived there at the end of the Cultural Revolution more than twenty years earlier.

When I arrived at the office, I was nervous. I was not familiar with the rules of business, or the language of business contracts—or even how to behave myself among businessmen. And I was wearing a dress I had bought at a Macy's basement sale, without any jewelry (I have never liked wearing jewelry), so I was afraid they would think I was a simple, poor kind of woman. Perhaps it was that I felt I did not have much time since I had research to do, or perhaps it was that I had grown accustomed to the more direct way Americans do things, but I just told them what we wanted to do, and said that if they thought they could do it, then sign the contract.

But they did not want to do business that way. They wanted to put me up in a hotel, invite me for lunches and dinners, things like that. It sounded like the negotiations would take several days, and I could not stay anywhere near that long.

So I said, "I am leaving today whether you sign the contract or not. I cannot stay longer. I have signed it already—are you going to sign, or not?"

I think they were shocked at my behavior, wondering what kind of woman I was. They signed the contract, so I suppose my direct approach worked, but we were never actually able to do any business with them.

One of my professors was Dr. CS. He was born in Shanghai as the son of a general, and his family came to the US in the early 40s, just before

America got involved in World War II. He went to Dartmouth and Columbia, then started teaching at Ohio State in 1969, where he became the first director of East Asian Studies. He was close to retirement age when I was his student. I took two classes from him, one of which was an independent study. In the other class, the regular one, he gave me a C on the first test in the first semester. Many other students got As, but he gave me a C. I had hoped to get his feedback on a paper, to improve my grades, but he refused to read it. Then he wrote a memo about my C grade and sent it to all the professors whose classes I was taking—including the graduate students' director, the scholarship committee members, and others. In response, the department changed my advisor to Dr. CH, who had just returned to campus from his two years' sabbatical. Soon after that Dr. CS retired.

My new advisor was Dr. CH, who was from Taiwan. His father-in-law, a high ranking nationalist, was caught by the Communists in 1949 and put in prison on the mainland. The rest of his family, like so many others, fled the mainland when the Communists defeated the Nationalist party (KMT) and established the People's Republic of China. When Chiang Kai-shek and his remaining troops and staff retreated to Taiwan and continued using the national title, The Republic of China, the relationship deteriorated even further: there was no relationship or communication between the two regimes at all. Each side claimed they were the legitimate government of all China, and there has been tension between them ever since. Even today, the Nationalist party still claims they are the legitimate government of all China, and until 1987, they were the only party allowed in Taiwan. But for several decades support has been growing to abandon any claim to mainland China and declare formal independence, and in 2016, the Democratic Progressive Party—which opposes the PRC's One China Policy—won the presidential election as well as a majority in the legislature. Anyway, people in Taiwan thought Dr. CH's father-in-law had been killed by the Communists, so they considered him a national hero, so his tablet was placed in the National Revolutionary Martyrs' Shrine in Taiwan. The National Revolutionary Martyrs' Shrine is a shrine in Zhongshan District, Taipei, Taiwan, dedicated to the war dead of the Republic of China.

Dr. CH immigrated to America to become a scholar, and after getting his Ph.D. at Harvard, started teaching at the Ohio State a year before Dr. CS did. He was an eminent scholar in Chinese history with a specialty in intellectual history and the history of political thought. He was a leading researcher, one of the first scholars to examine the inner dynamics of Chinese tradition in the New Confucianism movement, as well as cultural and intellectual transformation in modern China.

Dr. CH did, of course, have other students from mainland China besides me, and he became involved in some trouble I had with one of those students, Yaping. She was, in fact, a friend of mine two years ahead, who also took Dr. CH's classes and sought guidance from Dr. CH even though she was in a different department, Asian Studies. Looking back on it, I think she must have had some kind of psychological problem. Whenever she was unhappy, she would just start talking to someone and go on and on, non-stop, whether or not the person was paying attention. And most of what she said was just complaining. Maybe I listened too much, because I became one of her regular targets. She would call me several times a week and complain for hours at a time. Finally, when it came time for me to defend my dissertation—when I was busier than I had ever been—she kept doing it, and I just did not have time for that. I had to tell her how busy I was, but she still didn't stop. The only thing I could think to do was to stop picking up the phone every time, and only answer sometimes. She was unhappy with me for that.

There is a Chinese term for students who started earlier, *xue jie*. One day Yaping told me that Qin, my *xue jie* and another advisee of Dr. CH's, had badmouthed me in front of Dr. CH. I did not know whether to believe Yaping, so talking to Qin did not make sense. I thought the best thing to do was to talk to Dr. CH directly, so I went to his office.

I didn't tell him why I was there or what was going on; I just asked him, "Do you support me 100%?" What I did not say was that if he said "no," I was going to quit school.

He looked puzzled, of course, but he said, "I am your advisor, so of course I completely support you."

"Thank you," I said. And I left.

A few days later I was shocked to receive a long letter in the mail from Qin asking why I had badmouthed her in front of Dr. CH, and saying she didn't want to be my friend any more. I certainly had never done that, but I guess Yaping told her I had. I called her several times, but she never answered. I felt I had to do something, so my husband and I drove to her apartment. She was home, and though I was not sure if she would talk to me at all, she did open the door.

"You have a lot of nerve, coming here," she said angrily. "What do you want?"

"I know you think I badmouthed you to Dr. CH, but I didn't. I never said a single bad word about you!"

"Then what did you say? I know you went to see him."

"All I did was ask if he fully supported me. That's all."

She just stared at me. We had been friends, and I think she wanted to believe me.

"Why don't we both go talk to him together?" I asked. "Then you can hear it from him."

Qin looked down at the ground, then back up at me. "Okay."

We had to wait, of course, until he was available in his office.

"What can I do for you today?" he asked.

"You probably wondered why I asked you a few days ago if you fully supported me."

He nodded. "You weren't the only one to ask me strange questions this week."

"There are rumors about what we said about each other in front of you, that we badmouthed each other."

"I see," he said thoughtfully. "Let me reassure you that no one has spoken ill of anyone else. It is troubling that such lies can be spread so easily. Remember that it is more shameful to distrust our friends than to be deceived by them. Put the whole matter out of your heads."

We nodded, recognizing the Confucius saying.

"Is there anything else?"

Qin and I glanced at each other.

"No, sir," I said. And we left. She did eventually stop being angry at me.

In the last couple years of the program, the closer I got to graduation, the more hopeless I felt. I became depressed. Other students I talked to, especially Asian studies majors, all said there was no hope that a Chinese history major like me would find a job. They said the openings on the job market were for American history, European history, maybe general Asian studies, but nothing as specific as Chinese history. But I had to keep going even though I felt hopeless; I had even less idea what I would do if I abandoned my Ph.D.

When it came time to do my Ph.D. oral qualification examinations, I needed more people to fill out my committee, and Dr. Yan-shuan Lao was one of them. He belonged to the same generation as Drs. CS and CH —his family, like theirs, having fled to Taiwan to escape the Communists. Since he came from a distinguished family, his father being the eminent historian Lao Gan, he had received a classical Chinese education. When he attended National Taiwan University, he had the good fortune to learn from renowned scholar Yao Congwu (a.k.a. Yao Schi-ao). This top-notch education enabled him to go to Harvard in 1957 for his Ph.D. in East Asian Studies, and become an expert in the Yuan dynasty era. He established that the Mongols who ruled China during the Yuan period were not mere savage barbarians, but respected and preserved Chinese culture. He made such significant contributions to the study of Yuan history that Harvard invited him back to teach in 1976. Dr. Lao was widely regarded as an excellent teacher, and Ohio State was blessed to have him for several decades. He was truly a Renaissance man and a "living encyclopedia" to his colleagues, friends, students, and everyone who knew him. Dr. Lao was incredibly knowledgeable on many topics and in many fields, yet was not condescending. Whenever one of us (including his colleagues and friends) approached him with a question in Chinese history or literature, a particular event or personality in Chinese history, a phrase in a four-line Chinese poem, or a song lyric, or thorny issues of translation, he always had the answer right off the top of his head. Deeply rooted in Chinese classics, he was definitely one of the top experts in the whole country in Chinese history and Classical literature. To me, he was a true scholar, in every sense of this noble title, and was the epitome of the Confucian scholar, accomplished and wise yet humble, kind, noble, and courageous, concerned with the moral and cultural order of the world around him.

After my graduation, Dr. Lao continued to encourage and help me to publish, particularly to pursue and complete my recent book, Red Genesis: The Hunan First Normal School and the Creation of Chinese Communism, 1903-1921). In the long process of writing and revising this book, Dr. Lao helped me tremendously in many valuable and concrete ways with his sinological erudition. During our numerous phone conversations, most of the time I asked him questions; he was always kind and helpful, and he made me feel both at ease and motivated.

Dr. Lao was a fine poet. He wrote many beautiful verses in Classical Chinese style. However, he set his own high standards on poetry, as well as on research. When I urged him to publish his poems, he always felt that they were not good enough. When I admired a literary allusion or a certain sentence he used in the poems so beautifully, he always said that was very common. He said he memorized the literary allusions when he was young. They were all there in his mind and he just picked one up when it was needed. It was just that simple. Dr. Lao sent me his selected poems only after I begged and only the ones he felt could be presented. He only interpreted/analyzed half of them to me before his health deteriorated. Alas, I will never have this chance to hear his whole explanation of these poems.

It gave me a little bit of comfort that I mailed Dr. Lao and Shimu (Mrs. Lao) a short hand-written letter before he was gone telling him that he could never imagine what he has meant to me and in what profound ways he has influenced me. Dr. Lao and Shimu (Mrs. Lao) called me just a few days before he passed away that he was very happy to learn that.

At that time, like Drs. CS and CH, he was close to retirement. Since he was a professor of East Asian Languages and Literature, I had taken classes from him. But he was a morning person, while Dr. CH was a night person, so I did not know how to choose a time of day for my defense.

Since Dr. CH was my dissertation advisor, I decided to start by asking him.

"Why not do it in the afternoon?" he said. "That should be a good time for both a morning person and a night person."

It made sense, so I went to Dr. Lao to propose that.

"No, no, no!" he said, becoming agitated. "I have too much to do in the afternoon. I will find someone else to take my place."

Now, these were two respectable elder Chinese men with similar backgrounds. Dr. CH had been the first director of the East Asian Studies program, and was well-respected by students and colleagues, so it seemed to me that he was not afraid of anybody in his department, or even the college. But Dr. Lao was an expert in Chinese classics, and whenever Dr. CH had to translate something to do with the classics, he would have Dr. Lao review and correct his translation. So the relationship between them was complex.

I went back to Dr. CH to tell him how Dr. Lao had reacted. I thought it would bother him at least a little, but he just accepted it.

"Go ahead, pick a time in the morning. It's okay." He was behaving as though he were the inferior person of the two men. Or perhaps he found Dr. Lao intimidating. At any rate, that solved the problem.

To me, the Ohio State Ph.D. qualification exams seemed cruel compared to how other schools handled them. We were not allowed to bring any materials, but were ushered into a room at 8:00AM with only a table and a computer and had to write essays to answer five major questions. So I did not eat anything all day. I was able to finish before 5:00PM, when the office closed—although there were a lot of typos in my essays. I did not feel like myself when I left the room. The other Ph.D. students who had been taking their qualification exams looked relieved, like they had come back from death. But Qin, the student who started two years before me, had not yet finished her essays when 5:00 came. The school locked her in the room overnight. That gave her time to finish her essays, and she was allowed to turn them in, but I thought it was cruel.

It turned out that I did find jobs to apply to. One interview was at a school in California, and it seemed to go well. They said they would let me know within two weeks whether they wanted me or not. Everyone said what a paradise it was there, with strawberry fields and orange trees and lemon trees and so on, but I did not like it. The thought of living there for the rest of my life was so depressing. I knew in my heart I shouldn't accept any offer they made me. The offer I did accept came from Georgetown College in Kentucky. Later on, that school had financial difficulty, and the department chair, also a dear friend, who had hired me actually apologized several times on different occasions, "I'm so sorry to drag you in." In fact, I feel very fortunate to work at this beautiful institute. The spirit of unselfish love, justice, and compassion to which the Georgetown community is dedicated touched me at the very beginning of my campus visit. My meeting with faculty members of the History Department and others at the college left a deep imprint in my memory. I love my students and colleagues at the college and many of whom have become great friends over the years. Particularly, I feel so blessed to have Jim and Lindsey from the history department as colleagues and dear friends. They have been invaluable sources of intellectual guidance as well as reliable friends who were always there whenever I needed their help.

It was hard to leave Columbus after more than seven years of life there. When we had everything packed up and were getting into the car to drive to Lexington, Chris's friends, who were playing soccer in a playground down the street, all came running to say goodbye. He had tears in his eyes. We were all sad. I cried all the way to Lexington.

But I was not quite done with Ohio State yet. Although I had a job, I hadn't done my dissertation defense yet. On the day my defense was scheduled, I drove back there only to run into more drama. I walked into the room, and the only person I saw was one of my committee members (not Dr. Lao or Dr. CH).

"Where is everyone else?" I asked.

"We cancelled your defense. You are not ready."

Figure 6.1. Color photograph of Georgetown College's Learning Resource Center. From Georgetown College stock photo

Figure 6.2.   Color photograph of The Ohio State University's University Hall. From The Ohio State University

I did not understand at all, and did not know what to say.

I didn't sleep at all that night. The next day I called to ask for advice from a good friend, Yi who was a few years younger than me, yet I thought she was so intelligent.

"You should just talk to him," she said.

So I called the professor. "I was ready," I said. "Why did you say I was not ready? Did I do something wrong or offend you?"

He did not respond right away. Finally he said, "You complained about me to another professor."

I had no idea what he was talking about, but I certainly would never have meant to offend him.

"I am truly sorry," I said. We sorted it out. I did my dissertation defense as scheduled that day and did it well, with sincere congratulations and praise from every single committee member.

Yet I was still upset. Why had no one bothered to tell me before I drove there that the defense was cancelled? Anyway, I felt such a sense of relief after the defense.

CHAPTER SEVEN

A Single Plank

I went back to China last summer, and as I always do, I went with my siblings to visit my mother. I also spent some time with her alone, sitting on the ground beside her grave and crying.

My parents came to visit us in the States in late October, 2006. They stayed for several months with us in Lexington, and we planned a big trip for December to take them to see Las Vegas and the West Coast. But just before we were to leave for the trip, Mother found out that she had a malignant tumor in her bile duct. I went in to shock when I heard that, thunderstruck, my mind blank. For days and nights afterward, my heart was racing, pounding like sound of the drums beating in my chest, or like the thunder of guns trying to tear me apart. I had no appetite and could not bring myself to swallow any food. I felt my whole world was collapsing; I did not know how I could continue my life without Mother.

In January 2007, Mother and I went back to China for her surgery in Beijing at the hands of the best surgeon in the nation. The doctors said she had about a year to live. I went for a walk by myself after hearing that. As I walked along the Beijing streets, oblivious to the snow falling through the cold air and cars rushing past, I felt the most painful desperation. I was suffocating from despair. I decided to stay with Mother for another month, then return to the States. I wanted, and needed, to be with my husband and son, yet I did not want to leave Mother. If I said farewell to her this time, would it be forever?

So it was with enormous unwillingness that I eventually returned to the States. Before I left home—for China had remained my home even after fifteen years in the US—I hugged Mother tightly, wrapping my arms around her thin shoulders. I said something trivial, trying to keep my tone of voice relaxed, yet my heart ached like there was a knife twisting in it. I promised her I would come to see her during winter vacation. I did not let her see me off at the airport as she wanted; my brother and his family picked me up. I got into my brother's car and looked back at the small neighborhood courtyard and found Mother was standing there.

Her white hair was waving in the wind under a white birch tree. As the car began to move, taking me farther and farther from her, her loving gaze never faltered.

My eyes filled with tears. I was afraid my family would see them, afraid I would not be able to contain my feelings. I knew the parting had been just as difficult for Mother. I had seen in her eyes the love, tenderness, and attachment to her children. "Who dares to say that a weak grass can be reported for the spring sunshine on it?" is a saying that means, who dares to say that a child's filial piety can repay the mother's love?

When we talked on the phone, my second day back in Lexington, Mother told me she felt tired and had not gone out for exercise in the morning. Soon after that her health began to deteriorate, so her pain and suffering increased every day. By December, her condition was causing her severe suffering, yet she was afraid and unwilling to go to the hospital. I tried to coax her into going, saying that she only needed the hospital to reduce her inflammation and increase her urine output. Even though my family already had airplane tickets to China for the next month, I told her I would fly out to her whenever she needed me. I said, "I am your lucky star—as soon as I go back everything will be just fine." So she agreed to go to the hospital.

Despite her suffering, Mother had been strong throughout the year. Chris spent his winter break with us, and one day we called Mother to give her the good news that Chris had gotten an investment banking job with J.P. Morgan in New York City - but Mother burst into tears. Her cries were heart rending. My sister was there at her side, and tried to comfort her, but she continued to weep. My heart was breaking. I hoped a miracle would happen and she make it through the illness.

Mother only stayed in the hospital for two weeks. Then, on December 24, 2007, she left her loved ones forever and went to another world. I rushed home as soon as I could. She was lying there quietly, her eyes closed, her mouth a little bit open. She looked serene and kind just like she was sleeping, but she could no longer respond to my call. I thought about the pains she had taken to raise us, how she had supported us her whole life—and I cried my eyes out.

Mother had loved me, taken care of me, and raised me, yet I was not at her side at her last moment. What was worse, I did not honor my promise that I would go home to be at her side any time. This became an everlasting pain, like a festering wound buried deeply in my heart that smarts whenever it is touched. Family and friends all tried to comfort me.

"It was a relief for her, to leave so quickly," one said.

"It was a blessing that the illness and pain did not torture her any longer," another said.

I could not help thinking that Mother did not linger because she wanted to spare her children any more trouble. It made my heart ache unbearably to imagine her being in so much pain yet worrying about being a bother to us.

All those years, living in the US, "home" was still in China because Mother was there. Without her, where was my home? She had gone somewhere I could not go, and she had taken my home with her. From that time on, just like in the Tang poem by Li Shangyin, I had no more home, no clothing sent from home, no mother for my desolation, and I was alone in this world. The lamp of my life's genesis was extinguished.

It is not easy to make a living in a foreign land, and I often feel like I am walking on a bridge made from a single plank: there is no turning back and there is no time to look around. Despite all the years I had been in the States, first studying at universities, then teaching at college, Mother had never felt as distant as the many miles between us would suggest. We did not see each other very often, but we spoke on the phone daily, and that was the single plank on my bridge. Without it, I was falling helplessly into a seemingly infinite chasm.

The day Mother left was a cold winter rainy day, and the chill penetrated to the bottom of my heart. While I had heard the word "heartbreak," I had never thought of it as anything but a vague metaphor; now I felt that my heart really had broken into pieces and could no longer function. That winter I experienced the coldest, the darkest, the most depressing, and the saddest time of my life. I felt panic, loneliness, and helplessness as I had never imagined I could feel. Mother's affection, her love, her protection, her companionship were nowhere to be found. There was a hole where my heart had been—not just a hole, but an empty, boundless void. I was in a trance the entire winter. It often happened that I would suddenly realize I did not know where I was or how I had gotten there. I began to understand a deeper meaning in the saying that, no matter how old a man is—even if he is 80 or 90 years old—as long as his mother is still alive, he can still retain a childlike spirit. A man without a mother is just like a flower in a vase; although it still has color and scent, it cannot grow and is doomed to wither.

When I was young and cried hard, I would get a toothache so painful I had to take painkillers. When Mother passed away, I cried every day for hours, for six months afterward, yet I felt no pain—until one day when suddenly, in the middle of crying, the tooth pain came back and I had to take painkillers. Eventually my figurative heartache became real, physical pain in my chest. There were few other things I could do to escape the pain in my chest initially, such as reading a novel.

It was a long, long time before I was able to get myself out of a state of sadness. In fact, doctors diagnosed me with depression, which they said gave me "heartbreak syndrome" that caused this heart pain. And although I could not have imagined it when Mother left, my depression got even worse in the next few years as my family—already a small one—got smaller still and close friends, including dear former teachers, also left us. Especially Drs. Lao and Rife's passing away deeply saddened me and worsened my heart pain. My one remaining relative, Mother's younger brother, passed away a few years after she did. My sister's husband passed away suddenly, and as I listened to her daughter sobbing from heartbreak, it was too much to bear. In fact, after hearing my niece cry like that, my heart pain became so bad all the time that nothing would stop it, not even painkillers. It was unimaginably terrible.

There was constant misty rain the spring after Mother died. The rhythm of the peach rain, the apricot rain, the cherry rain, and the pear rain all wet the flowers, but also dampened my heart. Yet during that year's Qing Ming festival, Lexington saw not drizzle but heavy rain for three consecutive days. Torrential rain from the heavens to accompany the torrential tears from my eyes. You see, April used to be my favorite month; my life started in April. But after the lamp of my life was extinguished, April's new green, blooming flowers, fallen flowers, and drizzle, can only make me sad and tearful.

April rain promoted the blossoming of flowers in May. Flowering May ushered in Mother's Day—the first Mother's Day I didn't have a mother. I worked hard to avoid seeing anything that would remind me of what day it was. I felt so lonely, and any reminder would bring pouring tears and agony.

During those first months after Mother passed away, not a moment went by that I didn't miss her. I missed her while I was doing housework. I missed her while working at school. I missed her while laboring in the garden. I missed her on snowy days. I missed her when flowers first bloomed. I missed her when flower panels fell from the trees like rain. I traveled to try to distract myself, but still I missed her. I just could not accept the fact that the one who most selflessly loved me in this world had left me forever.

Before whenever I called home it was always Mother who picked up the phone. Now I would never hear her voice again. How would I face the cruel reality that she has really gone at the time when the whole family was getting better, when her children can carry out the filial piety? As Confucius said, when sons and daughters want to carry out filial duty, parents don't have the time to wait—what kind of words on earth can express the huge pain in my heart!

In my life until that moment, I rarely thought about the questions of soul and the other world, yet after Mother had gone I often thought of these issues. I believe Mother must have entered the kingdom of heaven with wisps of silver gray smoke curling and rising into the air, where she will have no more suffering and pain. When I am on an airplane, sitting in my seat, watching the quiet world pass by out the window, I cannot help hoping she will appear before me like a white cloud. Or like in Jody Foster's film *Contact*, when, moved by her character's perseverance and sincerity, the aliens assumed her father's appearance to speak to her.

How much I hope, and how often I fantasize, that mother could return from that quiet and distant world, either by taking the floating clouds, or stepping on the glittering stars, or riding the gusts of wind! I would say to her things like this. . . .

Alas, my dearest mother, how can I bear that you are gone forever? I am so attached to you. I long for you to stay, even your lifeless body. When the pouring tears covered my vision, I seemed to see your kind smile clearly.

In this flowering season, Mother, did you see the colorful flowers in our blossoming garden? Did you see the peaches on the peach tree? Did you see how exuberantly the trees and plants you trimmed have grown? Whenever I watched the weaving shadows of the trees and our flower garden, I thought of you and missed you terribly.

Come back, Mother, please don't leave me! How I yearn to talk with you and share everything with you—all the joyful things and all the annoying things. How I ache to walk in the park with you, go to the beach with you, wander in the forest with you, see the outside world with you, and enjoy the life you loved!

Although we are divided between heaven and the human world, how can this stop our connection? I know the light from twinkling stars is your love beaming from heaven, and the fresh breeze is your guardian from heaven. And I still hunt far and wide in the vast starry sky every night, and search through the seven-colored clouds every day, longing for your return.

II

Drinking Wine

CHAPTER EIGHT

A Touch of Elegance

My maternal grandfather was born late in the imperial era—which ended in 1912 after the Republican/Xinhai Revolution of 1911. That revolution occurred mostly because the Qing Dynasty had proven unable to keep foreign powers out of China or to modernize the country. As I said earlier, Grandfather was a scholar. At that time, education was synonymous with study of the Chinese classics, especially the *Four Books—the Daxue* (Great Learning), *the Lunyu* (Analects), *the Mengzi* (Mencius), *the Zhongyong* (Doctrine of the Mean), and *Five Classics—Shijing* (Book of Poetry), *Shu jing* (Book of Documents), *I Ching/Yi Jing* (Book of Changes), *Li ji* (Book of Rites), and *Chunqiu* (Spring and Autumn Annals), which together formed the basis for the Confucian tradition and the civil service examination during imperial China. During the Song dynasty, the Four Books were singled out by Zhu Xi and his commentaries became the standard curriculum for the imperial civil service examination system in 1313 and continued until the whole system was abolished in 1905.

All literate people, not just scholars, were expected to know these texts by heart. Grandfather was very good at calligraphy, and small print in particular. He could write very beautifully with the Chinese brush. Actually, all the traditional Chinese scholars were supposed to write beautiful calligraphy. Grandfather read and wrote every night under the oil lamp–a bowl with a cotton wick dipped in vegetable oil. Each night, he would only go to bed after the lamp went out without oil.

Grandfather's specialties were the *Book of Changes* (the *I Ching*) and books of traditional Chinese medicine. The *I Ching* is probably the most familiar to Westerners. It began in the Western Zhou period (1000-750 BC) as a divination manual, but over time, people came to find broader, deeper meaning in it, and the addition of scholarly commentary in 136 BC (the "Ten Wings") created the *I Ching* we know today. The basic way it works is that you generate six random numbers, find the hexagram (a stack of six lines that are either broken or solid) in the text that matches your numbers, then read the commentary for that hexagram. While there are more recent methods of generating the random numbers, such as dice and coins, Grandfather used the traditional method of manipulating yarrow stalks. Yarrow is just a flowering plant; I do not know how it came to hold this special role.

The *I Ching* can be used for something as simple as seeing a person's future, but serious practitioners like Grandfather try to see cosmological patterns and identify differing layers of symbolism. He would tell people before they got pregnant what to eat or do if they wanted to have a baby boy, and it was pretty accurate, so he was well-known for that. He lived in Old Town Luoyang and we lived in the western part, so about 10 *li* apart. Whenever he wanted to visit us, he would consult the *I Ching* to determine the best time to go.

Grandfather had one habit which everyone thought was weird. He lived with my uncle, along with my uncle's son, two daughters, and wife, who was a nice person. They made a certain noodle dish that was his favorite, so they would bring a bowl of fresh noodles to him in his room, and he would put it on the window sill—right next to several other old bowls of noodles. He did eat them, just not right away. He always ate the oldest one, even if it was moldy. Sometimes the mold would be over an inch high. He would just push the moldy hairs away and eat. I have never understood how he could do that, but he never got sick. He always told us how long he was going to live and when he was going to die. In the end, Mother said he died by accident.

But he passed away at the age of 90—the age he had always said he would die. A few years after I left for the US, we found out he had taught several students the I Ching. One year while I was visiting, staying with Mother as I always did, my cousins (my uncle's children) came to visit.

As we greeted Hongda and Laoli, I could tell they had something they wanted to tell us.

"Where is Haohan?" Mother asked.

Laoli laughed. "He said he ate some bad noodles, and now he's sick." She sat down.

"Bad noodles? Grandfather would be ashamed of him," I chuckled.

"Maybe," Hongda said, his eyes twinkling, "but he'd be proud of his students."

"Oh, his students are all old now," Mother said.

"That's what we thought!" said Laoli.

"Several young people came to see us yesterday—" Hongda started.

"—and they said he taught them—"

"—fortune-telling!" they both finished excitedly.

"That old slyboots!" Mother exclaimed. "Why would he keep that a secret from his own family?"

"What did they think of the fact that he was wrong about his death?" I wondered.

"We don't tell anyone that," Mother said. "What good would it do?" She wandered off.

"How could he have had secret students?"

"It wasn't like he stayed at home all the time," Hongda said.

"And he was kind of famous," Laoli added. "People sometimes came to our house to ask if he would teach them."

"Now his students are well-known fortune-tellers in Old Town."

"At least, that's what they say!" Laoli laughed.

Mother returned holding out a small pouch. "Tell Haohan to drink tea made with these herbs. They will redirect his qi."

As I said, Grandfather also specialized in traditional Chinese medicine, so while Mother never studied medicine, she had learned a lot of secret prescriptions of traditional medical treatment from Grandfather. Mother relieved the pain of so many people and cured many complicated, seemingly-incurable diseases. She was especially good at curing epilepsy and hernias. My husband graduated from Henan Medical University and was a Western medical doctor in China, and these two diseases he did not treat himself, but referred patients to Mother to treat. For those two diseases, patients fully recovered. It was amazing. Western medicine could not solve those problems, but some herbs could.

She did this all voluntarily. Whenever some friends, neighbors, colleagues, or relatives did not feel well, they often came to Mother to ask what to do. In her last year, I went back three times to visit her. One night I went out with her and people were still asking her for help, like one man who asked what to do about the poison scabies on his back, or the woman who wanted to know what do about her serious heel pain. So Mother was really like a guardian. She worked hard, to protect people around her, make them safe, and relieve their pain. Mother enjoyed a good reputation and prestige among all the people who knew her.

It was no accident that she worked so tirelessly to help people, because she was a devoted Buddhist. She was registered at *Baima si*, the White Horse Temple in Luoyang, as a Buddhist disciple. According to legend, White Horse Temple was the first Buddhist temple in China, established in 68 AD by Emperor Ming of the Eastern Han dynasty, whose capital was Luoyang. There are several versions of how it happened, but here is one of them.

In the tenth year of his reign, the Emperor dreamt he saw a divine man with a body like gold and a shining sun and moon behind his head, descending from heaven to the front of the Emperor's throne, and then entering his palace.

The next day, Emperor Ming told his advisors of his dream.

"It was a most impressive experience," he said. "I felt as though I were in the presence of a divine being. Tell me, what does it mean?"

A minister on the Board of Astronomical Calculations, said, "Your Majesty, I have heard that India possesses one who has arrived at perfect wisdom, and who is called Buddha. It must have been his body flying with divine radiance through space that was the origin of your dream."

Another scholar said, "Your Majesty, early in the Zhou Dynasty, during the twenty-sixth year of the reign of King Zhao, there was a great earthquake. The creeks and rivers overflowed their banks and the entire land shook. The astrologer Su You consulted the *I Ching* and determined that a great sage had just been born in India who would transmit a teaching which would come to China after a thousand years; clearly now is the time for that teaching to come to China."

"I have never heard of this Buddha before," said the Emperor, "but if now is the time for his wisdom to reach us, then we must assist him if we can."

So he sent a delegation off to India to learn about Buddhism. As the story goes, they met two Indian monks in what is now Afghanistan, and convinced them to return home with them along with a book of scriptures, relics, and statues. The *Sutra of 42 Sections* is the text the monks created for their new Chinese Buddhists. It contains passages from various Buddhist books, but compiled to mimic the Confucian Analects so that the Chinese would be more comfortable with them.

As the story continues, since the monks travelled on two white horses, the Emperor had a new temple built in their honor the following year. We do know for certain that the temple existed as early as 258 AD, and almost four hundred years later, during the Tang dynasty, a famous monk named Xuanzang travelled to India to learn more about Buddhism. He came back sixteen years later to White Horse Temple with many Buddhist scriptures. While serving as the abbot of the Temple, he translated the scriptures from Sanskrit to Chinese. Of course, like so many ancient buildings, most of the original temple was destroyed at various times, so the current buildings were constructed from the Yuan Dynasty onward.

White Horse Temple was so important to China that in 1961, the government made it one of the key historical and cultural sites that is under state protection. Without that protection, it may have been badly damaged during the Cultural Revolution.

Obviously, by being a disciple at White Horse Temple, Mother was part of an ancient tradition. Of course, she practiced meditation, recited mantras, and so forth—but for her the most important was compassion toward all living beings. All her life, she embodied Buddhist compassion.

When I was little, we lived in a shabby one floor apartment that was home to three families. Not only did we share one kitchen, but the kitchen gate was the door to the outside, so to come or go you had to pass through the kitchen.

Now, when I say kitchen, you must remember that while we had electricity for light and running water for washing, we did not have any appliances: no refrigerator or stove or dishwasher or toaster or anything like that. It was a simple room. There were shelves, of course, a sink, and a long wood-fire brick oven with several holes on top to set cooking bowls in. There was a table to set food on, but we did not eat while sitting on chairs formally arranged around the table as is common in Western countries. I would not want to live without electric appliances now, but there was something more inviting about the atmosphere of my childhood kitchen.

I remember one winter morning, so early it was still dark, and so cold it was snowing outside—winters in Luoyang can be cold, but are usually very dry, so snow was not common. I was in the kitchen with Mother, when we heard a voice from outside.

"Hello?"

We recognized the voice; it was Old Song, the milk delivery guy. In those days, milk was delivered in the early morning for babies to drink when they awoke.

Mother hurried to the door.

"Come in, come in!" she said as she opened it.

He hesitated.

"It is too cold to stand around—come in! You must be frozen."

I watched him as he nodded gratefully and hurried in. He looked so cold.

Mother picked up a cup and went to the stove. She filled the cup with hot water from a pot and handed it to him.

"The stove is warm," she said. "Come warm your hands."

With a smile, he set down the milk bottle to take the cup of hot water, and I noticed how white his hands were. They were wrapped in rags because gloves were not something the government considered worth producing.

He stepped over to the stove, and it was such a beautiful scene: the red-hot flames flickering in the stove, the yellow light they gave off lending a warmth to the whole room, and the man with his hands stretched out over the stove. His hands warmed quickly.

The government did not like to admit it, but at that time beggars were common. Some people were mean to them, but whenever a beggar came to our building, Mother always invited him inside, gave him a seat at our table, and fed him. She would feed him even though we did not have enough food for ourselves. And before he left, she would give him food to take with him, such as steamed bread.

She tried hard to provide tasty food for us, even when rationing made it hard to get much food. My favorites were fried beltfish—named because it is shaped like a belt— and fried twisted noodle, which was crispy and sweet and impossible to forget.

Mother was a talented sweater knitter. She could reproduce a sweater from just a picture, and people always admired the sweaters we wore. She also enjoyed operas of all kinds, and loved to travel. She was so curious about the world and eager to learn about different cultures. One of her favorite things to do was visiting mountains with Buddhist temples. She carried incense when she traveled, for her own observances, and when we encountered a temple, she would always worship there. She also loved growing flowers and various plants. I remember that she grew a kumquat tree, three Chinese toon trees (a type of mahogany used in Chinese traditional medicine, with young leaves and shoots that are eaten as a vegetable), and snow beans.

I have no memory of Mother ever complaining. No matter how hard life was, how hard the day was, how hard work was, not a single time did Mother complain. Instead, she was always optimistic and satisfied—no regrets at all.

This beauty of character matched her personal beauty. She was so beautiful as a girl that no one ever used her real name; they just called her "beautiful girl." One time when I was little, we went to see one of the rare movies the Communists allowed, and all I can remember about it is that the beautiful actress on the screen looked just like Mother. And I was not the only one who thought so—everybody who saw the movie said, "it's your mother!"

I think the women in my family have been growing less beautiful, because my mother was more beautiful than I am, and according to my sister, Grandmother was more beautiful than Mother. But it wasn't just physical beauty that made her stand out. She had an elegance and grace to her. Even as she aged, and became short and bent over, and her hair turned snow white, she never lost that quality. Her friends thought it indicated an aristocratic temperament, and it could be that it came from her family background, since her parents came from gentry families.

Mother was so brave and strong, so optimistic when she learned she had cancer. She loved life so much, and had an instinctive desire to survive, so after she had surgery, her health gradually recovered. Of course, in the end, the cancer took her life, but we had several months together in China that were beautiful.

My biggest wish on this trip was to take Mother to see Kaifeng or Xian. When I told her on the phone that I was going back to see her in late September, she asked me: "how many days left for the end of September?" From that time on she looked at the calendar every day and counted how many days left till I would arrive home.

I went back in late September and Mother had recovered very well. Her spirit was very good while I was there. Every morning we walked five or six li before breakfast. After lunch and breakfast she and I would also walk around for a while in her neighborhood. We spent a lot of time just chatting, or watch TV together. Sometimes my brothers and sister came, and we played cards with her. It all made me so happy.

In mid-October I accompanied Mother to visit Kaifeng, which was the home town of her ancestors—yet she had never been there. She was very happy in Kaifeng. She was so excited she could not sleep the whole night, yet she was still in high spirits the second day. We visited almost all the attractions in Kaifeng. I've been very grateful to my friends Yan and Qun whose help made this trip very successful.

Even after Mother passed away, in the midst of the anguish I suffered from, I sometimes felt her presence. One time I was sitting at a table in Coffee Times Coffee House on Regency Road, Lexington when my cup of tea suddenly moved toward me—and I heard her say, "Take some tea." It is a comforting thought that she is still around caring for me.

CHAPTER NINE

A Raincoat Made of Straw

Many people seem to think Chairman Mao's Great Proletarian Cultural Revolution was either bad or good. If you are reading this book, you have probably read about the Cultural Revolution elsewhere, and you already know the hardship and loss it caused me. But the truth is, I enjoyed a lot of it. I do not think there were any second graders who were sad that school was cancelled. I was thrilled, getting to hang out with my friends all day and never have to do homework or study or sit still in class.

Now, the Long March was a pivotal experience in the formation of both the Communist Party in China and the leadership of Chairman Mao. In October, 1934, 130,000 Red Army soldiers retreated from the Kuomintang in Jiangxi Province, in southern China. Because the KMT controlled half a dozen areas of southern and central China, the Red Army chose to travel west to Yunnan, and up through the mountains of Sichuan and Gansu Provinces, before arriving in Shaanxi. Only one tenth of the force made it there a year later. This experience was held out to us as, basically, the hardest thing anyone has ever done—so whenever we were expected to do something hard, we could not complain because our revolutionary leaders had endured the Long March. But it was also a source of inspiration: if they had accomplished something that difficult, surely we can accomplish whatever we set out to.

One spring day two of my classmates, Big Nose and Miao Jianxiu, came to me and asked, "Do you want to form a Little Red Guard group?"

"Yes!" I said. "We should go on a long march, to prove our dedication."

By now, Big Nose had seen Jianxiu's obvious fervor for the revolution, so while he still called her a capitalist roader sometimes, he was only teasing. The fact that, as different as they were, they both wanted to form a group, was compelling to me.

"Just like my older brother's Red Guard group did!" Big Nose said, beaming excitedly.

"Let's go to Wangcheng Park." Jianxiu said. "Maybe something will be going on there." Wangcheng Park had been built about ten years earlier. At almost 100 acres, it has a lot to offer: a zoo, cultural history, giant peony gardens, an amusement area, and more. It was not so fancy back then, and everything had been made to serve the revolution. But sometimes there were movies, and it was a popular place to organize events.

So we marched east along the main street of the city. This was during the "wheat rain," in late May, when we had left the chill of winter behind for good, but before the full heat of summer took hold. It rained, we got wet, and we didn't care. The walk was several miles, and we were only nine or ten years old, so it took hours. We entertained ourselves by singing songs, chanting slogans, telling jokes, gossiping, and so forth. Eventually we reached Wangcheng Park, but didn't see anything interesting happening. I wanted to look at the ruins of Wangcheng—a city built in 1021 BC early in the Zhou Dynasty as the new capital—that had been partly excavated within the park. But Jianxiu and Big Nose made fun of me for being interested in Old Culture, and we were all really tired. So we just walked home. That was my only Long March during the Cultural Revolution. Looking back, it says a lot about those days that these little kids were free to wander so far from home without any adults even knowing they were doing it.

When school started again, I was so enthralled by Chairman Mao that I enjoyed all the political indoctrination—the chanting and slogans. I have heard from Christians in the US that they enjoyed singing songs at church camp, so perhaps it is easier for us to find enjoyment when we are younger, no matter what we are doing. Or perhaps I was just brainwashed.

But I enjoyed a lot more than the school activities. Beginning in middle school, we often went to the countryside to help the peasant farmers to do some farm work, especially during the harvest season. As I said earlier, our school was attached to a factory, and at the end of each month, we always went to the factory to help the workers. I felt very excited to do those things.

The factory had three shifts: day shift (8 AM to 4 PM), second shift (4 PM to midnight), and third shift (midnight to 8 AM). I do not remember that we ever worked the third shift, but we did work the second shift— and that was my favorite. During our break at night, we would go outside and crowd around one classmate who was an excellent storyteller. She sometimes told scary stories, and I enjoyed those, but we listened closely to every story she told.

The first year of high school we had no regular school, but worked the entire year at the factory, Luoyang Bearing Factory which was and still is one of the two huge government run bearing factories in the country. Our school was attached to the factory. It turned out that not only was I good at academic learning (perhaps not surprising considering my family background), but I was a good worker too. I got so good at the work, that my worker teacher (Shi fu) taught me how to do everything with the machine—and then did not need to be there. Whenever anyone needed something, they brought me the drawings and I could make exactly what they needed.

From a Western or modern Chinese perspective, our factory would have seemed a strange place. There was no supply and demand to drive our work, since the government decided what and how much to produce, and their priorities were always politically-oriented. Sometimes we had nothing to do because there were no orders. Other times we could not meet the orders due to shortages of parts or materials; it did not always occur to the party leaders that someone else had to make this part so that we could make that product. And occasionally we would meet an order but the products would sit around because there were no trucks available to transport them.

My second year of high school (remember, high school was only two years), I spent three months in the countryside as a tractor driver. I also learned how to assemble a radio. The first time I did it successfully, my friends wanted to use the radio. We wound up using that one to listen to as we worked. Eventually it stopped working properly, but until then we could listen to several stations. I heard that sometimes people could hear counter-revolutionary radio broadcasts, from somewhere unknown, but we never heard any.

We could get Central People's Broadcasting Station, of course, plus Radio Peking and a few others. Everything was chosen or sanctioned by the government, so it was not like listening to the radio here. And some of what was broadcast we could have heard anyway, because loudspeakers had been installed throughout the country, in cities and in the country-side, on telephone poles, treetops, and rooftops, so that everyone could hear important broadcasts like Chairman Mao's speeches. But the radio stations did play music, and news—and mostly we just felt like we were slightly more a part of the modern world.

In addition to being trained to do things we actually did, we took classes to learn how to do things we might need or want to do, like being a barefoot doctor. That class was hard for me because I was terrified of needles. At one point we were learning how to do acupuncture, and it was my turn to be demonstrated on; we all took a turn as the patient both so that we could understand what the patient experiences, and so that we could see the differences between patients. But no one was ready for what happened when it was my turn and the teacher stuck the needle in between my thumb and my index finger—he could not pull it out! My muscles were so tight from fear that the needle just stuck in there. Every-one laughed, and I had to admit it was funny. I do not remember how the teacher got it out; maybe someone had to massage my hand. I left the class shortly after that.

During my first year in high school, Deng Xiaoping had been allowed back into politics as First Vice-Premier. One of the changes he implemented was education resurgence, which just meant that some schools were chosen to return to classroom education rather than working in the fields or the factory. My high school was Number One High School, and as I have said, it was attached to the factory. In my second year of high school, Number Two High School had three months of education resurgence, and I went that school to join the math classes. I was also a member of the school basketball team. We got up very early in the morning for long distance running and jumping, and to practice playing basketball.

The moment the trucks came to take me and my classmates off to the countryside was one of the best moments of my life. When I look back at it, I see a brainwashed youth, but that does not change my experience at the time. Jianxiu and I thought we were the luckiest, happiest people in the world. The rest of the world, to us, was suffering in deep water and hot fire. If we worked our hardest to make China strong, we would be able to liberate Taiwan and people around the world from their suffering. We sincerely believed that, and our efforts to become the heroes our country needed got us through the hardships of the first two years, until Chairman Mao died.

But it wasn't all hardship. With as little as the people in our mountain village had, they still shared with us sometimes. Well, many of them were kind to *me* anyway. One spring day—late enough in spring that grass had started to grow again, but early enough that there was nothing to harvest—I had been so hungry for so long. I sat on the ground, holding my stomach because it hurt. The sun was strong, and the air was still and hot. I stared at the ground in front of me, watching a beetle climb over the blades of grass. I recognized the grass, *Jicai* (shepherd's purse). Supposedly people in southern China thought it was delicious. In desperation, I grabbed a handful and shoved it in my mouth. As I chewed, I did not think it tasted good, but it was not bad either, and I kept chewing.

"What are you doing?" yelled a voice nearby.

I turned to see an old man hurrying toward me. We called him Old Tian. He was too old to run, but I could see he was really trying.

"Don't eat that!"

"It's better than nothing," I said.

He was breathing hard when he reached me, and I was surprised to see tears in his eyes.

"You do not need to do that," he panted. He bent over and grabbed my hand. "Come!"

"Where?"

He pulled me to my feet.

"Come with me."

Old Tian tugged at my hand, and I followed him. He led me to his house. "Come in and eat."

"Oh, no," I protested, "you do not have to—"

"You must eat." He pulled me into his house.

No one in the village had much, but this man was even poorer than most. He had almost nothing. Yet he went to his stove and poured me a bowl of soup.

"From now on," he said, "whenever we have a bowl of soup or some food, you will have some too."

Old Tian was so nice to me. But he was a noble man in general. On rainy days when we could not work in the fields, everyone stayed home—except for him. He would go out in a hat and raincoat made of straw, and walk around the fields to see if anything needed to be done, like draining a water buildup.

I have never forgotten his kindness. After I had been in the US for a while and could afford it, I tried to find out his phone number—not that he personally had a telephone, but at the very least the village had one. It was a lot of work. I could not afford to call China very often myself (especially since I was already talking to Mother every day), so I had to write letters and ask people to help me. Many people were either unable or unwilling to help, and I ran into dead ends too. But eventually someone wrote back with a phone number I could use to reach him.

I was a little nervous as I sat down with the telephone, and contemplated calling him. Would he remember me? Was he still alive? It would be so sad to do all this work, only to find out he was gone. I took a deep breath and dialed.

"Wei," a young woman answered.

"Hello, this is Yee He calling. I lived in your village for three years during the Cultural Revolution, and if Old Tian is still around, I would like to talk to him."

"He is so old!" she said with a laugh. "I wonder if he'll *ever* die." She must have pulled the receiver away from her mouth then, because she yelled, "Hey, go get Old Tian, would you? Tell him He Yee wants to talk to him"—but it wasn't very loud.

"It'll be a while," she said. "He's really slow. Sorry, I don't remember you, but I was just a little kid back then."

"Of course," I said. "How is his hearing?"

"Oh, it's fine. And he still gets around on his own."

We chatted a few more minutes, till she finally said, "Here he is."

"Wei," said a voice that was familiar, but even raspier than I remembered.

Figure 9.1. Watercolor painting of a raincoat made of straw hand. From Liu Shuyong pen name 老树画画 (laoshu huahua)

"Hello!" I said eagerly. "It is so good to hear your voice."

"I remember you, Yee. So many of the young people who came to live with us were worthless, but you were one of the good ones."

"I have never forgotten your kindness to me. I would never have expected—"

"Psshhh!" he dismissed my praise. "To see the right and not to do it is cowardice."

"Thank you."

He grunted. "Are we done making each other uncomfortable now?"

I laughed.

"I do not think you would recognize me," he said. "I am even shorter!"

"Are you the oldest in the village now?"

"Oh, I do not keep track of such things. I ache just the same either way. But enough about me! Tell me what life has brought you since you left us."

So I told him about going to university, teaching, starting a family, and moving to the US. He was still such a nice man. Talking to him made me realize that, for all the *zhiqing* suffered, in the end we got to go home, have careers, travel, and benefit from the tremendous improvement in China's standard of living over the last forty years. The villagers have not.

One of the few advantages the villagers had was that families were much more likely to stay there for generations (rather than moving around), so that even the poorest person had family to take care of them. There was one old woman who did not have any relatives, and was taken care of by the village. We called her Wu Bao Hu, a term for the rural poor who have no spouse, children, or parents, or are unable to work, and who received a subsidy according to the Chinese Constitution. I suppose from an American point of view this would be like calling someone "Poor Subsidy Lady," and may seem callous, but Chinese are much more accepting of and flexible with nicknames. And comparatively, there are so few Chinese family names that we have to get creative in order to distinguish people.

Like Old Tian, she was worse off than the rest of us, so on good days, when we had enough wheat flour to make two steamed breads, I would secretly take one to her. I tucked the bread into my clothing so no one could see it, and went through the village as I would normally, but when no one was looking, I ducked into her house. I had to be so careful because many people would think it was a waste to give her food that we could eat.

One autumn day about a year after I arrived, a strong wind was blowing as I walked back from working in the fields. The air was cool—the first real cool spell of the season—and it felt good since I was hot and sweaty from working hard.

I heard someone calling my name, and looked around to see Jing hurrying toward me. She looked upset.

"What is it?" I said, worried. "What happened?"

"It's Wu Bao Hu," she said sadly. "She collapsed suddenly, and she's been calling your name."

We ran toward Wu Bao Hu's house in silence. The barefoot doctors could not do much for old people once they started to decline; they did not have much equipment or access to any medicine beyond the basic stuff. And, as I said, many people thought the elderly were taking up resources that were better used on healthy, productive people. This attitude may have predated the Communists, but the scarcity and rationing imposed on the villagers by the Communists certainly made it worse.

As we reached Wu Bao Hu's house, a barefoot doctor emerged looking somber.

"How is she?" I asked, feeling that I already knew the answer.

"She is gone," he said.

Jing took my hand. I knew she was sympathetic to those who felt that there wasn't much to go around and we should be smart about how we use it, so we could contribute our best to the country. But she was my best friend, and she supported me.

"She really called out my name?" I asked.

The doctor nodded.

I was sad, of course. But the fact that she wanted to see me, when she knew she was dying, meant that I had made a real difference in her life, and I took comfort in that.

Despite the miles between us, Jianxiu remained my best friend throughout my time in the countryside, but I also became very good friends with several other local girls in my village. On hot summer nights, the river was the coolest place to be. We would stroll down to it laughing and talking loudly, so boys would know that girls were bathing and playing here in the river and would not come nearby (how pure the villagers were at that time!). Other nights we would climb up into the white pine trees. We liked the white pines because they symbolized long life and we found that comforting. Up there, in the breeze and the darkness, the girls would take turns telling ghost stories. I was so scared, but really loved listening to those ghost stories. I'm still obsessed with ghost stories to this day. Those summer nights in the village were some of the most enjoyable moments in my *Zhiqing* life.

Ghost stories are different in Chinese culture because, unlike the dominant American idea that the spirits of dead people only linger when they have unresolved business, the traditional Chinese belief is that the souls of all people continue after death—that is the normal state of things. In that sense, Chinese spirits are not supernatural. In fact, the idea is that there are two parts to the soul, corresponding to the yin (instinctual) and yang (reason) aspects, and each type of spirit would haunt people in a distinct way. There are a series of rituals, from mourning to the funeral to burial, and even to continued veneration, that must be performed. Most of the time, these things are done, and the spirits continue on their way to the underworld (which is simply where they live). A ghost is usually a spirit that has been prevented from continuing on to the underworld by the living, who have not done their duty.

But Chinese ghost stories also feature demons and monstrous spirits, and those were my favorites. There were the *Yaoguai*, shapeshifting demons who trick their victims so they can eat souls and become immortal. There were the "hungry ghosts," borrowed from Buddhist tradition, restless spirits of people who had excessive desires in life, or who died a violent death; they were hideous creatures with big stomachs, green skin, and fiery breath. One girl's family had raised her with Pu Songling's Qing dynasty-era collection of folk tales, *Strange Tales from a Chinese Studio*, and she exposed us to many ghost stories that are now considered classics. I was scared but fascinated by it all.

My enjoyment of those storytelling nights was not just about the tales themselves. I felt that it was a beautiful thing to have those moments when we could forget our harsh circumstances; it also reminded me that, as hard as life was then, at least no one was haunting me!

I didn't mean that the "Up to the Mountains, Down to the countryside" movement was not a mistake. Even though I didn't exactly have much use for the new skills I had picked up in the countryside, like cutting wheat with a sickle, winnowing grains with a wooden spade, and plowing the fields with oxen, I knew that I was capable of doing all of these things well and this somehow gave me a safe feeling at the bottom of my heart. I knew that I was not just a professor. I was once a farmer and a worker too. I could support myself in the countryside if it came down to it. I felt I had received *duanlian* (*temper*) from the difficulties and suffering in the countryside. *Duanlian* (*temper*), a metallurgical term, is often used figuratively referring to *zhiqing* in their difficult sent-down years who had improved their resiliency like fire in a furnace tempering steel. At the end, it turned out just like the greatest Taoist philosopher Lao Zi's saying: "Good fortune breeds disasters. Misfortune ushers in well-being."

I talked about Jianxiu's leukemia before that she got after we had been in the mountains for a year. The timing of her death was so strange: here I was, finally returned from the countryside and excited to go to a real school again, and my best friend was suddenly dying. But I thought the way she dealt with her disease was so brave, so full of grace. She had actually gone into remission for a year before that. Now she needed multiple injections every day, and they had to be given at five o'clock in the morning. Because she had worked so hard to understand what was happening to her body, she knew she needed the medicine. Though she had an IV for fluids, for some reason they could not use it for these medicines, so every injection was separate. After a while, scar tissue built up around her veins from all the injections, and the nurses had to work harder and harder to get the needles into her. It must have been painful for her, and the nurses felt bad about doing it. But she always smiled and reassured them, "It's okay, don't worry, just go ahead and do it." I was so touched by the way she faced death with consideration for others, and with laughter.

At her funeral, Jianxiu's parents told me the story of what she had done the night she told me she was leaving. After hearing her say that, of course, they had refused to leave her side, so they were still there at midnight.

"Please, pull out all these tubes I'm connected to," she said.

"What? Why would we do that?" they said. They knew that without the tubes, she would die quickly.

"Please, just do it for me."

"No, you need them!"

"I know, but I'm begging you to pull them out."

They looked at each other with tears in their eyes, beginning to understand. So they started to pull out the tubes, and as they did, they also started to cry.

"I'm sorry, please put them back in."

"What? But you said—"

"I know, but please, now I want you to put them back in."

Confused, but beginning to accept that she was not going to explain herself, they did. And they all settled in for the night.

The next morning:

"Please pull the tubes out," she said again.

"You said that last night," they said, thoroughly confused now. "But when we did it, you said to put them right back in again."

"Last night," she replied, "you started to cry. You were disturbing the other patients who were sleeping. Now they are awake."

They began to cry again, but pulled out the tubes, and she passed away very soon.

When I heard that, it reminded me of Charlotte Brontë's novel *Jane Eyre*, and the conversation Jane has with Helen before Helen dies, when Helen invites Jane to nestle up against her to get warm. Helen is so peaceful in the face of death, and believes she is just going to her last home. Jianxiu seemed just like Helen to me, concerned not with her own imminent passing, but with the comfort of the people around her.

CHAPTER TEN

The Pride of Heaven

After returning from the countryside, I went to Henan University in 1978 to major in English. I might have chosen that field of study anyway, but the government saw English as one of the keys achieving the Four Modernizations (economy, agriculture, scientific and technological development, and national defense), so there were special incentives to study English.

That was a time of rapid change in China. In December, Deng Xiaoping became "paramount leader," which can be confusing for foreigners because it is not a position or official title. Chairman Mao was, for a while, the official head of the state, the party, and the military, and there was a desire after his death to avoid that kind of concentration of power. Deng was not the head of state, the party, or the military, but he was the man in charge. That same month, US companies began to do business in China, and on January 1, 1979, the United States recognized the People's Republic of China. A few months later, Deng made an official visit to the US. All of this paved the way for him to institute major reforms.

As a result, the early 1980s were a golden time in China—it was quite liberal. The government allowed more free expression for a while. People in general, and especially intellectuals, were encouraged to express their thoughts via articles, poems, and etc. I think it was a reaction to the severe restrictions during the Cultural Revolution and the mind-control techniques that Chairman Mao had used.

My college years were also a golden time in my life, in part due to the general atmosphere of freedom, but also because I discovered how much I loved academic work. Big surprise—I was a scholar like my ancestors! It was quite a sudden change for me, to go straight from the physical hardships of the countryside to the life of a student in a big city, where my survival was not at stake. I discovered that I wanted the same thing most English majors I knew wanted: to study in the US, to see what it was really like there. I would lie on my bed fantasizing that someday I could live there for a few years. I read many books about students in the 1920s,

30s, and 40s, who went to the West to study; eventually most of them became well-known scholars in their fields. That was an inspiration to me. I would get together with other students with the same desire, and we would talk about what we knew about America, and where we wanted to go if we got there.

I think it is difficult for many American young people to imagine how out of reach the goal of studying in the US seemed to us. There were so many obstacles, from our political records—which were sometimes wildly inaccurate and largely beyond our control—to how expensive it was just to travel there, to being so far from home, to how relatively few people were approved to go.

But we had excellent teachers; they were the best of their generation, I think. I studied Japanese as my second foreign language, so I remember that we had three Japanese instructors, one who had grown up in China, and two who were graduates of Japan's most prestigious university, the Imperial University. Another teacher I had for intensive English reading, who was quite young, had graduated from the language department of Peking University. And we had an American as well. She married a Chinese student while he was studying in the US and then came back to China with him. She became very famous in China. She was even interviewed by Chairman Mao. All our teachers were responsible, worked hard, and cared a lot about our studies.

Despite all that went wrong with the Cultural Revolution, I think we still understood that the intention had been to improve our country, and that desire did not disappear just because the Cultural Revolution was a disaster. So now we felt like we were doing something concrete to help bring China into the modern era. Everybody seemed to feel happy. People looked up to us students and called us the Pride of Heaven.

When I graduated from Henan University in 1982, I was assigned to Luoyang Teachers College to teach English, as well as survey courses of British and American literature. To be assigned to teach English was not surprising, given the need for it. Of course I had wanted to go back to Luoyang, but there was no guarantee since the government decided all that, and I was delighted when I was assigned there. I discovered that I love teaching. I was only five or six years older than my students, so they saw me more as an older sister—and they loved me. Even today I am good friends with them.

I taught at Luoyang Teachers College for six years. As I said, the fact that I was not interested in joining the Party made it difficult for me to become an Associate Professor. Fortunately for me, the president of the school liked me. He was a real intellectual, renowned as a literary figure and a critic—and he was a former Rightist. He rejected the idea that political fitness was the most important trait in a teacher. He talked to the school's Party Secretary and the leaders of my department, to say that I was doing an excellent job and he didn't understand why they were not promoting me. They said to his face that they would pass me, but when I showed up for the meeting to approve me, they rejected me again. He had to intervene again, then they rejected me again. And we went through that process a third and a fourth time! Only then did they promote me.

One day I was riding the bus—few people had cars back then, so buses, bicycles, and walking were the ways most of us got around—when I saw two of my students get on. Since this bus did not go to the school, but did go by Wangcheng Park, I figured they were probably going there. We greeted each other, and as I watched them together, I realized that they were lovers. It was not as obvious as it would be in the US; they were not touching. But when two people love each other, they cannot help behaving differently, and of course I had seen them each on campus, so I could tell the difference.

They had to behave differently on campus because back then, college students were even not allowed to date. The official reason was that dating would distract from their studies—which were considered one of the keys to modernizing China. But even today, the Chinese government limits the discussion and expression of anything sexual, and the Chinese Communist party has always valued chastity. These students probably felt that they were being careful by being together only when they were off campus, without considering that other people from school might see them on the bus, or at the park. I thought it was a beautiful thing, the picture of both of them together, even though I could only see it on the bus. I was somehow very much touched by the beautiful picture of both of them together. I did not report it to the school.

Being a teacher, and then an Associate Professor, did pay a bit more. So when I got married to a doctor, we talked it over and decided our incomes together gave us enough money that we could afford to raise a child. And we had a son, Chris.

Meanwhile, more economic and academic reforms were announced. Religious freedom was restored. And some developments associated with the West came with those changes: inflation, corruption, prostitution—and the political unrest which later led to the Tiananmen Square massacre.

After the Hopkins-Nanking Center opened in 1986, I was fortunate to be one of the few admitted to the graduate certificate program two years later. I thought it was a beautiful campus, and of course it was brand new. Built in western style on the edge of Nanking University, it was a huge building in three parts, with five floors and three sections—all surrounded by walls. It included housing for the American professors, classrooms, an open-stack library (rare in China at that time), and a cafeteria.

No outsiders were allowed inside. Chinese have always loved building walls around buildings. Every school, hospital, factory, company, kindergarten, every unit was surrounded by walls. And Nanking University is in the old city of Nanking, surrounded by walls built at the beginning of the Ming era when the city was the capital of the new dynasty. So many walls!

Building on my years of learning and teaching English, I decided to study American history and American culture. I also took the TOEFL, which the Center encouraged all Chinese students to do, so they would know how good my English was. As I said, the school worked hard to mix Americans and Chinese together, so I had an American roommate, Priscilla. We quickly became good friends. Of course, we did not have much time together, since we had to work so hard. But it was still a wonderful life, and having her made it less painful for me to be apart from my husband and baby, who could not live with me on campus.

Priscilla and I did enjoy being interviewed by David Holley from the LA Times. He came that March to do an article on the Center, to highlight it as a major sign that China really was opening up. Priscilla was very kind to me in her interview; she said "I have a great roommate" and "she's made all the difference in my stay here." Though he did not include my name, it meant a lot to me that Mr. Holley used those statements in his article.

The appeal of studying in the US eventually proved to be stronger than the pain of being separated from my family for a period of time, and I decided to apply to schools there. I would have had a hard time knowing which schools to choose, but a good friend from Johns Hopkins Nanjing Center, Ling, whose fiancé was studying at Penn State, recommended four schools in the US for me to apply to. Like me, she was determined to get there (and she did—she is now a history professor in the states).

I mentioned earlier how expensive it was for me to apply to those four schools. But I didn't have to pay that cost, because Priscilla generously paid the fees for me. And her mother volunteered to sponsor (mainly like a financial sponsor) me for the student visa I would need to study in the US; I gratefully accepted the sponsorship, but paid for the visa, tuitions, and all the living expenses at IUP myself. In the end I chose IUP mostly because I already had two connections in Pennsylvania: Ling and her fiancé, and another Chinese woman, a good friend of mine who married an American man she met at the College in Zhengzhou where they were teaching. Priscilla's family was not far away either, in New York City.

Once I had been accepted by IUP and decided to go there, I had to get my student visa—and that meant I had to go to the US Embassy in Beijing. I was fortunate to be in Nanking, on a major rail line, so the trip did not take too long. I say "not too long," but of course this was before the bullet trains, so it still took almost 24 hours. I took the train north, through Xuzhou, Jinan, and Tianjin. From the railway station, I took a bus to the Chaoyang District, where the most of the foreign embassies were located. The current US embassy compound was built in 2008; in 1989, diplomatic relations had only been re-established ten years earlier, thirty years after the previous embassy had moved to Taipei in 1949 when the Nationalists fled there.

The Hopkins-Nanking Center, although it was created in partnership with an American university and featured American professors, was still mostly designed and run by Chinese. So the US Embassy was my first experience with an American bureaucracy. To explain part of why that was interesting to me, you have to understand the "Iron Rice Bowl" policy. After the Japanese invasion during World War II and the Chinese civil war, the country had horrible inflation and money became worthless. When the Communists took over, they appealed to the people by guaranteeing jobs: we will give everyone a job, and everyone will get paid the same no matter how hard they work. In the short run, this was successful because it almost eliminated unemployment, homelessness, and other social problems. In the long run, it left employees with no concrete incentive to do a good job, and although in 1986 the government did away with permanent employment at state-run offices, the people who worked in those places were still known for being lazy and unhelpful, and for doing bad work when they did work (believe me, it was much worse than anything I have seen in America).

So as I walked into the Embassy, I was curious to see what it would be like to interact with the bureaucracy there. And overall, it did seem to be run better. Not all the employees were equally helpful, but it was obvious they were all doing work.

When I was let in to see the visa officer, I got out the LA Times article. I had brought it with me because I thought, who knows, maybe it will make a difference. I gave him my paperwork and the application fee, and he looked it over, muttering to himself as he made sure everything was in order. Then I handed him the article. That got his attention! He could not take his eyes off it. He had to answer the phone twice, and his assistant interrupted him once, but each time he went right back to reading the article. Then he approved my application and told me to pick up my visa three days later. I was, and have always been, so very grateful to Priscilla and her family for their help.

After I finished my one-year program at the Center, I went home for the summer. Many of my former students were still around, and I offered to give them extra lessons on weekends. Since the classrooms were only open on weekdays, when they were full of students taking classes (yes, even in summer), I decided to teach my classes—mostly intensive

English reading—outside, under a big tree on the Luoyang Teachers College campus. It was very hot, of course, but few Chinese buildings had air conditioning at that time, so the difference was not as great as it could have been.

CHAPTER ELEVEN

A Wild, Vast Moor

I was terribly airsick and still feeling horrible when I first arrived in America. It was not until about a week after I arrived at IUP that I stopped feeling sick to my stomach, and was able to appreciate where I was. After class that day, I walked around the campus just to take a look. It was a beautiful sunny day, and the air felt delightfully dry compared to what I was used to in Nanking. I started at the north end, where many of the residence halls are, and quickly decided I liked the feel of it. Some parts were prettier than others, with flower beds and lots of trees, while other parts were more open, but it was all neat and clean. The brick buildings felt welcoming. Then I came to the Oak Grove, which is like a park inside the campus—big enough that I could forget I was at school—with a lot of shady trees. The Grove quickly became one of my favorite places on campus, as was true for many students, and I made a point of going there every day, even if I only had time to walk through it. The trees there were older and taller than most other trees on campus, and I could feel the difference. I loved to lie down there, feeling the grass on my back and my legs, the wind on my face, and look up through the branches at the sky. Sometimes I would see hawks circling overhead, and there were usually several squirrels nearby, scolding me.

When I reached the other side of the Oak Grove, I came to the libraries. What a marvel it had been the first time I saw *two* libraries, one containing special media and children's books, and one for everything else. The idea of a media library was new to me because there were so few electronics in China back then. Next I walked through another set of residence halls. It took me weeks to learn what all the buildings were because so many were long ones; while they may have a sign at the entrance, that didn't help me most of the time when I approached from a difference direction. This area was fairly new and did not have many plants, so it felt a bit stark. After a few more academic buildings, I came to the sports area on the south end of the campus. I spent very little time there.

The whole campus was much bigger than Henan University, Luoyang Teachers' College, or the Hopkins-Nanking Center (although the Center was on the Nanking University campus, which is quite large). I think its size helped make the campus feel open, but it was more than just size. There were no walls, and the students seemed more relaxed and able to have fun, compared to what it was like in China—which was not surprising when I discovered that most did not work as hard either! It took me a while to understand that whereas, at that time, going to university in China was an honor, and students generally felt that they were making the country stronger, in the US it was almost taken for granted. So many people here go to college after high school just because that is what you do.

I felt good about having taken the time to explore this place that would be my home for the next two years. The fact that IUP is in a fairly small town in eastern Pennsylvania meant that my introduction to the US happened differently than I had imagined. I had been excited to fly into New York City and stay there overnight, but once I got there I had not been able to leave my bed. Perhaps that was for the best; New York may have been too much all at once.

There were so many things I had to learn when I arrived at IUP. Of course there were plenty of everyday things that were familiar, but Americans and Chinese do a lot of things differently. I had to rely on Priscilla to tell me how to do what I needed to do; she was like my "back door." She spent a lot of time on the phone with me, and she was always patient and kind. She went even further by making calls for me where she did not know the specifics—such as calling the housing office to get advice and recommendations for finding an apartment to rent. I have talked to many immigrants, and also to Americans who have lived in other countries, about learning a new language. Everyone agrees that it is one thing to learn the basic language of daily life, but even when you are familiar with that, there are so many specialized areas of life (medicine, different kinds of businesses, etc.) that have their own language, and you have to learn those too. Priscilla repeatedly assured me that I could call her collect any time, no matter how late at night or how early in the morning. I was so touched by her friendship, and it made me thankful I had chosen IUP instead of other schools. I suppose she would still have been able to help me by phone if I had gone to a different school, but it made a difference knowing she was not far away.

At the end of the first semester, Priscilla's mom—my "Mom Armstrong"—bought me a round trip ticket from Pittsburgh to New York City. So I flew to New York to stay the first Christmas in this country with the Armstrongs. Since my airsickness had kept me from enjoying New York the first time, this was a wonderful experience. At that time there were some tall buildings in Beijing, which was the largest city I had been to in China, but it was nothing compared to parts of New York like Midtown or the Financial District. This was one of the places my fellow students at the Hopkins-Nanking Center had most heard about and dreamed of going. Since the Armstrongs lived across the street from Columbia University, they took me on a tour of the campus, which I thought was beautiful—all those grand old buildings. While China had many buildings which were much older, this place represented a tradition of learning and respect for academics which my home country did not have; as I said, scholars were looked down upon in China after the communists took over the country, especially during the Cultural Revolution, although scholars were on the top of the social ladder for centuries before 1949. Even now, I think scholars are more valued for their contributions to making China a great power than for their contributions to human learning and culture.

It was also quite a different experience to stay with the Armstrongs. I was much poorer in the US than I had been at home, and I spent much of my time with other poor Chinese students and families. But the Armstrongs were well-off, and while it felt so strange for someone else to be paying for everything, I was grateful that I was able to have that many experiences I would never have had otherwise. It was the perfect break from the endless hours of hard work, loneliness, and poverty I had been through that semester.

So I had my first Christmas Eve and Christmas morning, and the Armstrongs were nice enough to give me a few gifts. Gift-giving at birthdays has become more common in China, but generally Chinese give gifts throughout the year, to thank people or say goodbye to them, or when meeting people you are going to form a new relationship with, dinner at a friend's house, and so on. The general American idea of Christmas was familiar to me, but I did not know what it really meant to people; I was interested to learn that it varied a lot. I liked the focus on families and friends getting together, and seeing dear people who had been apart the rest of the year. I also felt sad for all the people who either lived too far from their family so they could not afford to travel, or who did not feel close to their family and did not want to be with them for Christmas. In China, while our immediate families tend to be smaller due to the one child policy, we do not tend to move around as much back then, and are closer to our extended families. I have a hard time imagining some Chinese refusing to go to a family gathering because they "don't get along" with their family.

After Christmas, the Armstrongs rented a big van and we all drove together to Boston to attend the wedding at Harvard University of one of their friends' sons. That friend was a famous professor in the Psychology department, so it was not surprising that many of the guests taught at Harvard; I remember meeting a number of famous historians, which was exciting since I wanted to teach history. While Harvard is not in Boston itself, we stayed for several days in a hotel (Priscilla and I shared a room, which was fun) and had time to go into Boston. I was fascinated to see another big American city, and the ways it felt similar to and different from New York. I enjoyed the varying styles of buildings; when I left China, there were so many squat, ugly newer buildings that contrasted with the beauty and elegance of traditional Chinese buildings. It was warmer in both places than it had been at IUP, but overall the weather that winter was fairly mild.

Then we took a train back from Boston to New York. Mom Armstrong was so thoughtful— she said they wanted me to experience all the different ways of getting around, so I would be more comfortable using them, and that was why I had traveled by airplane, by road, and by train. The only sad part of the trip was that Priscilla had to leave a day before I did, to get to her job on the West Coast, but I got along well with her parents and still enjoyed the next day with them.

Christians played a role in my life that I could never have expected. One of my friends, Joy, I thought of as my angel. She let me stay in her room the first night at IUP. She is a devoted Christian, and was a member of one of the dozen or so Christian students organizations on campus. She invited me to join, and I participated almost every week. I think she hoped that by being part of their group and participating in activities with them, my soul would eventually be saved and I would become a Christian. I thought they were all such nice people, and just enjoyed having something to do besides study. And they valued compassion and kindness in a way that reminded me of Mother.

One Sunday, as Joy picked me up for church, she had a question for me.

"Every spring and fall, we have a retreat in the mountains. A retreat is kind of like a spiritual vacation, where you go someplace special with other like-minded people, usually out in the country, to pray and think and bond together. Would you like to join us?"

"Yes, I would like to," I said. "Thank you."

"Now, it does cost some money to register, and I'm guessing $40 is more than you can afford right now, is that right?"

$40 sounded like so much money to me! I just nodded, embarrassed that I was so poor.

"Okay, well let me see what I can do."

"Thank you."

The next day, she called me.

"Don't worry about that registration fee. You're welcome to come."

"That is very kind of you," I said gratefully.

She never did explain whether she just paid it herself, or if she called the leaders to explain my situation and got them to waive the fee. I never did ask her. I was happy to go on the retreat with them, despite how embarrassed I felt at being so poor.

When the weekend came for the retreat, she picked me up and we drove south to a camp in the Appalachian Mountains. I did not think they were big enough to be called mountains, but I liked the long ridges and valleys. By now I had seen several different parts of the Northeast, and I was struck by how much of the land was undeveloped—houses and farms here or there, but so much forest. Since I had lived in central China, where people had been living and farming for 4,000 years, there was very little land that was not being productively used already. The fields and small towns in Connecticut and Massachusetts, which I had seen with the Armstrongs as we went to and from Boston, had felt different from the fields and small towns of eastern Pennsylvania, which I had seen while being driven to and from the Pittsburgh airport. The green rolling hills of the Appalachians were different yet again. They seemed so pretty to me, yet there were so few houses. I wondered why more people didn't live there.

While going to some kind of camp seems to be an experience many Americans have, often when they are young, I had never been to one—nor had I even heard of them. Seeing all the little cabins scattered around in the middle of nowhere, I was reminded of the village I had been sent to as a *zhiqing*. Although there were plenty of differences, when I thought of those three years from this perspective, my time in the village had been kind of like going to camp in one important way: I formed close relationships with the people I lived there with.

It was a beautiful area with lakes and meadows and trees, and this was my first fall in the US. The weather was warm and dry, with some morning fog. These days China has fall foliage tours too, but when I left home, few people had the time and money to be tourists in their own country. So I was amazed to learn that people would travel to certain parts of the US just to see the trees changing colors. It was a beautiful, startling view. So many different colors, from light yellow all the way through orange and red to almost a purplish-red. I spent a lot of time walking on the trails around the camp, and enjoying the time we were allowed for quiet reflection.

I was surprised to discover some apple trees, and one day when I was sitting underneath one, a couple apples fell down. I felt like Isaac Newton, but I was glad not to be hit on the head. I picked up one of them. It looked like a good apple, so I took a bite, and it was very tasty. I looked around at the other apples lying on the ground and wondered why no one was picking them up. I imagined that my son was with me, playing under the apple tree, picking up apples with me. I did that kind of thing a lot in those days, while my family was so far away. What would my son have done if he were with me now? What would my husband have said? That was the first of many neglected fruit trees I have seen in the US, their fruit left to rot by people who paid for that same kind of fruit at the grocery store.

There were other Christians I became close to. Pastor Murphy and his wife Dorothy were nice, friendly people who played a big role in my life while I was studying at IUP. I went to their church every Sunday, and they helped me a lot. For example, Pastor Murphy wanted to pick up my son and husband at the airport when they arrived here. Although another friend was the one who went instead, I was grateful to have so many people who wanted to help. The Murphys' oldest daughter studied in Tennessee, and then worked in Lexington, KY. So one time after we had moved to Lexington, they came to see their daughter and visited us too. They were happy to see that we were doing well because we had bought a big house. They are very nice people, and God bless them. I hope they have been doing well.

I became friends with two of Joy's friends, who were in her Christian student group. John and his sister, Chris took me to visit my friend Becca from college, the one with an American husband, Ed working as a special teacher. They were now married and living in eastern Pennsylvania. Both Becca and Ed are devoted Christians. They even home-schooled their two beautiful daughters all the way to junior high school. Both of the girls went to the best Christian college in the country and graduated with honors. Both of them have since been happily married and one just gave birth to a baby boy. I spent most of my holidays at IUP with Becca, and every time John and his sister would drive out of their way to drop me off with her.

We would leave school in the evening, after finishing our schoolwork, and sometimes it would be nighttime already when we left, and later than 10 PM with they dropped me off at Becca's. As I sat in the car on the way there, looking out the window, I always noticed how many big trucks there were. Being a truck driver seemed like such a cool, mysterious job because I did not know where they were going, driving here and there, back and forth all the time. I was so curious. The same was true, to some extent, with everyone in cars and buses too. I always wonder where they are going. Or if I pass a street, even while walking along, I wonder where that street leads—if I were to travel that way, where would I end up?

Anyway, John and his sister are such beautiful people. John is remarkably handsome, like Michelangelo's statue of David. People would often say to him, "you are so handsome," and he always replied, "it's my parents' fault." His sister eventually married another IUP student who became a medical doctor. John became kind of a pastor, doing the Christian good work, sometimes overseas, sometimes here. I hope they are all doing well and have a truly wonderful life.

My son Chris did not know any English when he arrived here, so I taught him his ABCs. I started by getting a lot of books from the library, mostly children's books, and I read them aloud to him. That seems to be a normal part of many Americans' childhoods, but it was not familiar to me from growing up in China. He listened well, and I felt so happy. It seemed like he was learning, so after a while I asked him to read some books by himself—ones with a lot of pictures and few words. I basically tried to give him his kindergarten.

So that fall he went to the first grade at our local elementary school. I spent a lot of time studying with him. I slowly brought him books with fewer pictures and more words, and more complicated stories. The following spring I decided he was ready, and found a library book to give him that was about a hundred pages—without pictures.

When he came home from school that day, I sat down with him.

"I have something special for you." I tried to make it seem like I had a treat for him.

I took the book out of a bag I had hidden it in. He took one look at it, and his eyes widened.

"Why don't you read this one next?"

He shook his head vigorously. "No, no, it's too big. How can I read that much?" He stared at the book, which was thicker than any of the other books I had brought home for him.

"Well, I'll sit right next to you, and whenever you come to a word you don't know, I will explain it to you."

Then I told him a bit of the story, and he perked up.

"I think it would be fun for you to read." I held the book out to him. "I know it looks like too much, but I know you can do it."

He took it from me slowly, still staring at it.

"Some day you will read many books that have hundreds of pages in them, just like I do." I paused. "You want to find out the rest of the story, don't you?"

He nodded.

"Will you read it?"

He nodded again.

And that was the real start of his reading English. From that time on, he read thousands of books.

Like other boys, he came to love reading military books. He learned about World War I, World War II, the Korean War, the Gulf War, and earlier wars as well. And he learned about weapons and things like that. He discovered authors that became his favorites, and he read all the books written by those authors. In those years he must've read several thousands of books. Now, even today, he still has the habit of reading. Even when he was working at Wall Street in banking, when life was so intense, he kept the habit of reading thirty minutes a day. Sometimes he did not have time to read thirty minutes, and he would make it up on the weekends. I feel so grateful that he has this reading habit.

Anyway, at the time I was teaching him, we may not have had much money, but we all felt happy to be together. I thought that life was full of happiness, full of hope, and the future was bright.

And good things were happening to us. Becca, of course, became a good friend because we both went to the same university, but as I spent more time with them, her husband Ed, also became a dear friend. They had an old red Nissan that wound up with a dent in the driver's side door, and they decided to give us the car, for free as previously stated, by transferring the title to us. We could never otherwise have afforded a car, and we were so excited to get one suddenly. To celebrate, we bought some bread and vegetables such as cucumbers and tomatoes, then we drove up to Niagara Falls and spent the day there. We had heard of those great falls, of course, but we were so happy to see them in person.

When I was learning English in China, I remember studying the fact that English has different words for an animal and for the meat that is eaten from it, like deer and venison, or cow and beef. I never imagined that "Beef" would be someone's name. Remember when I decided I needed a cheaper place to live, but didn't want to live with cockroaches? The place I found after that one, where I lived for the next year until my family arrived, I rented from a woman named Beef.

As I said, that was not her real name. When she was learning to speak, she could not pronounce "Elizabeth"—the closest she could get was "Beef," and somehow the name stuck with her. She was such a kind old lady. She had been a nurse in World War II, so she was in her seventies at the time.

She did not charge me rent as I mentioned earlier, which I was so grateful for. Her house was close to school, which made life easier for me. I did some cleaning for her, since I was living there for free. Many evenings we would sit in the living room, just chatting, trading stories, talking about our lives and our friends' lives, that sort of thing. She taught me a lot.

Beef had a big two-story house on School St., white with dark green trim. It had originally been her grandfather's house, then passed to her uncle before becoming hers, so it had been in her family for three generations. It still seemed new to me, so they must have taken very good care of it. It was the kind of house that made a big impression on me when I first arrived. The houses in Indiana seemed so beautiful to me, compared to how shabby the houses in China were at that time. I also remember noticing that around the town was just wilderness—you could not see more people. Even Pittsburgh, 56 miles away, seemed metropolitan to me back then. Now, of course, high-rises and other modern Western-style buildings are common in Chinese cities.

Anyway, Beef had a large yard with big beautiful trees in front, while the back yard had a garden and a grape vine—not much lawn. She grew mostly flowers and some vegetables, and was glad to have me to help her, since she did not have as much energy as she used to. She wanted to do more than she could, often saying things like "I need to take care of my garden, tidy it up," but it was not very neat. I did not have any knowledge of or experience with gardening, but I helped as best I could.

Even when my family arrived and I had to move out, Beef continued to be a mother figure to me. My son called her Lao Lao, which is what you call your maternal grandmother. I loved her, and she continued to help me after I moved out. Since I finished all my required classes in the first year, I was able to focus the second year on the research and writing for my master's thesis. Beef read my first draft and gave me feedback, and in January she told me she had really enjoyed reading it.

Even after all these years, I still remember one Christmas when she wore a light blue turtleneck shirt. I told her I thought it was such a beautiful color, and I just meant that it looked beautiful on her—but she bought one for me. I still have it, even though I wore it out.

I stayed in contact with her when we left Indiana. For many years I kept in touch with her, but eventually I did lose contact. Some other friends helped me try to find her, like checking with nursing agencies, and we searched for several years, but never did find her. Maybe she moved in with one of her children when she could no longer take care of herself. Of course, she would be very old now. I really hope she is alive and well.

I mentioned that when my family arrived in the US, we moved into a couple rooms above a garage; that was Mr. and Mrs. Mike's house. Like Beef, they did not charge us rent; I would never have expected so many people to be so kind to us. At first we let my husband's business calls go to the home phone, but we discovered the hard way how expensive those long distance calls were; we planned to pay the bill, but they said "No, no, don't worry about that. Just be careful in the future." They had grown daughters who called sometimes, and when I would answer the phone, they would joke with me, "Hey, there's a thief in the house!"

Their house seemed like a mansion to me, with two large floors and a huge yard. It was a brick red that looked good with the dark grey of the roofing. I said earlier that we lived above the three car garage, but it really was a separate house, painted yellow with the garage on the first floor and a small courtyard between the buildings.

Mr. Mike was a judge. His wife was an artist, and I think that is why the yard was beautiful. It was not just the large, pretty trees—the yard was dotted with lovely metal statues that she made. Sometimes they would have parties, and I always loved sitting outside in the yard, talking with such wonderful people. At one party, Mr. Mike brought out several bottles of wine, which was a new thing for me. The food was delicious, and my husband and I both enjoyed it, but neither of us drink. So when Mr. Mike poured us little samples to taste, we did taste them, but we just could not tell the difference! He said they were all very good wines, and of course I believe him; it's just a pity we could not tell.

They lived near a golf course, and one of Chris's favorite things to do was to go there when nobody was playing and pick up all the golf balls that were left behind. I do not know why he liked them so much, but he did. Some of the balls had been hit so badly that they were not even on the golf course—they were in my favorite place of all, because between the golf course and our house was a large undeveloped patch of land. I would take Chris there after school and we would just wander around on it. To some people I suppose it was just full of weeds, but to me it was a wild, vast moor. It made me think of the landscapes in stories by 19th Century writers like the Brontë sisters and Jane Austen. In particular, I had read about the town in Yorkshire where the Brontë sisters lived, and this wild land next to us looked a lot like how I had always imagined the Yorkshire moors. Like the Oak Grove at IUP, it was a place I could go to think and enjoy nature. And because this land was just behind our house, it was easy to get to.

So Chris and I would wander around looking for four-leaf clovers, which are also lucky in Chinese tradition. If we found some, we would bring them home and put them in a bottle with water, just as though they were pretty flowers. Of course, we also brought home actual flowers of different sized, usually yellow, white, blue, or pink.

After such a long time being so far away from my home and family, I now felt I was the happiest person in the world with my baby and my husband around me. We were together, although we did not have money. We could not afford to buy real fresh flowers, but I felt that those clovers and wild flowers were as beautiful as the fresh flowers in the florist's.

CHAPTER TWELVE

Guardian Angel

Dr. Merle Rife was a true gentleman. I met him as a student when he was teaching history at IUP, but he became a father to me and a grandfather to my son. He was born in Bloomington, Indiana in 1925, which made him just old enough to serve in the last several years of World War II, where he was a bomber pilot for the Navy. After the war he taught as a flight instructor for a year before enrolling at Muskingum University in Concord, Ohio to study history, and graduating in 1950. His father, who had the same name, taught Greek and Bible there. Dr. Rife got his master's degree at the Ohio State University and taught high school history for three years before starting to teach at IUP in 1958—the same year he got married. He went back to Ohio State to get his Ph.D., graduating in 1964, then stayed in IUP's history department until he retired in 1994. I always thought it was funny that he wound up in a city with the same name as the state he was born in.

He was quite an active man, serving as the president of the Indiana County Tuberculosis and Health Society, playing an important role in founding the St. Andrew's Village continuing care retirement community, and being a leader in the Four Footed Friends Animal Shelter, the Southwest Pennsylvania American Lung Association, and the J.S. Mack Foundation. Four Footed Friends was a no-kill shelter, and their work was very important to him. He helped them start a low-cost spay and neuter office in Indiana County, worked his way up to President of the Board, and only retired from that position when he turned 80. He somehow also found the time to work as a pilot for Indiana Airways from 1972-89. France was his favorite place to go, so he and his wife went there every year.

In the fall of 1991, I was just one of his many new students, but for some reason he took care of me—and my family too, once they arrived. We were one of three families from China that he took under his wing. I often think of those families by the children, since they were Chris's friends. Charlie was a few months older than Chris, while Larry was two years older.

When I started classes, there were at least ten professors in the department, but I could not tell the age differences between them. Now I know some of them were in their 40s, even in their 60s, but after I graduated, I told Dr. Rife how in the beginning I thought everyone was in their 40s—including him. He was actually much older than most of the others, and he laughed so hard. He was happy I had thought he was that young.

I worked very hard for him in class, and got mostly As. When he found out how poor I was, he started lending me textbooks for his classes. Sometimes I made copies of them, but other times he would let me keep the books for the whole semester. I did get a B- in one class, and there was one exam I got a C on. I was so shocked when he handed the exam back to me that I burst into tears right there in class, in front of him and all my classmates. It was so embarrassing.

The day my family's flight arrived from China, there was about a meter of snow on the ground. I got a surprise phone call from him.

"Let me drive you to the airport to pick up your family." He knew they were coming, because I had been so happy about it I told everyone.

"Oh, it's okay, you do not have to do that. Pastor Murphy said he would take me."

"Do you know what he drives?"

"Some kind of sedan. Nothing fancy."

"You need a vehicle that can handle all the snow on the roads. My Jeep has four-wheel drive, so it'll be safe." I knew he had a red Jeep because he had given me rides in it.

I hesitated. I did not want to offend Pastor Murphy, but I thought Dr. Rife was making a good point.

He seemed to pick up on my concern. "I'm sure Pastor Murphy will understand if you tell him you're worried about road conditions. You don't want your family to get stuck on the side of the road on their first day here!"

He was right about that! "Okay, I will tell him. Thank you so, so much!"

And he was right—Pastor Murphy was not offended, and Dr. Rife's red Jeep did very well in all that snow. He got us all back to Indiana safely, and dropped us off at Mr. & Mrs. Mike's place, which he had also found for us; he was good friends with them. I do not think he said anything to them about the rent. I assume it was their idea not to charge us anything.

We gave Chris a couple days to recover from jet lag before going to school. Dr. Rife wanted to drive him to school and pick him up from school, which I still think was remarkably kind. He was already doing so much. In fact, Chris had heard me talk about Dr. Rife so much that when he came home from school the first day, he said "Grandpa took me to school." We did not tell him to call Dr. Rife "grandpa"; that was his idea. Neither my father nor my husband's father had been part of our lives in China, so Chris had not had a grandfather, and I guess he had really wanted one.

He got a bit of a scare that first day. Since it was not just his first day at a new school, but his first day of school in a new country, Dr. Rife went into the building with him.

But then, as they were standing in the hallway, Dr. Rife said, "Wait right here."

And he walked away, back out of the building. He had just gone back to his Jeep to get something, but Chris did not know that. He thought, "Oh, Grandpa left me alone here," and he was frightened.

When he saw Dr. Rife walking back into the building—which was just a few minutes later—Chris ran up to him and held onto him tightly.

Dr. Rife knew Chris did not speak much English, so the best explanation he could give Chris was to hold out the note I had written to the school, so they would know Dr. Rife had our permission to drop Chris off and pick him up.

Then with his big, warm smile, Dr. Rife took Chris by the hand, and Chris relaxed. He still remembers that first day he went to school with his grandpa. There were only a few times Dr. Rife could not take him to school in the morning because he had early classes, and then his wife did it; she also picked him up from school sometimes. She was Chris's grandma.

Mrs. Rife was tall, pretty, and in good shape—even though she was a few days older than her husband—so they made quite a couple. She was a librarian at IUP when I started there, but retired just before I graduated. She had received her master's degree from IUP, so she let me borrow her gown for my graduation ceremony.

The Rifes' house was on the west side of Indiana, up on a hill overlooking the town; at night I loved to look down the hill through the woods at the lights of the town. They were so pretty. The house had its own well for water, which fascinated me. Since it was right next to the woods, families and small herds of deer visited their huge yard every day, sometimes as few as two, sometimes more than half a dozen. They had six indoor cats, and also put food and water out for the feral cats that roamed the area. At one point more than ten cats were coming to their yard to eat. Another time we visited them, and they had a kitten that had been born only a week ago. It was so tiny it fit in the palm of my hand. After graduation from IUP, we often came back to visit them. In the first few years after we left Indiana, we always stayed at their house when we came to visit them. In the last few years of Dr. Rife's life, we made sure to visit them every year. After Mrs. Rife passed away, [Mrs. Rife's health was much poorer] we went to visit him every year, at least once a year. Each time, we took him to a restaurant he picked for lunch and to some streets and campus buildings of fond memories. I also called him at least once a week, although he could not remember my name in his last year.

They had a son, John, and a daughter, Roseann, and Roseann worked in Washington D. C. at that time. It made them so happy when Roseann came to see them. Not like sons, daughters would chat with parents, especially with mother while helping her with cooking and cleaning.

Dr. and Mrs. Rife took us—and each of the other two Chinese families they supported—to Washington DC, and stayed in a hotel for several nights so we could see all the museums. Chris loved planes, guns, weapons, and military things like that, so his favorite part was going to the National Museum of the United States Navy, which had his grandpa's airplane on display. Even today he remembers which one was Dr. Rife's. Since our trip happened while Roseann was working in DC, we all had dinner at a Chinese restaurant in Chinatown.

During the last year of my master's program, I had many conversations with my professors about my future. My thesis advisor was Dr. Cashdollar (yes, that was his real name), and he gave me the advice that made the most sense to me; he said, "If you want to stay in this country, you should probably major in Chinese history." So that was how I chose my doctoral program. Dr. Rife drove me to OSU at least twice that summer, once for interviews, and another time to look for a permit.

Even after we left Indiana for Columbus (Dr. Rife was the one who rented the U-Haul truck to move our stuff), we often went back to visit the Rifes. I remember when my son graduated from college—which was about fifteen years after we left Indiana— we drove him all the way from Lexington to New York. We stopped by Indiana to see Dr. Rife and took him to lunch at a good restaurant. We also wrote them letters and sent presents for Christmas.

One day about halfway of the first year of my doctoral program (I had scholarship starting the second year of my doctoral program), Dr. Rife called me, and as we were talking he asked me, "Did you register for next quarter?"

"No, I am really tired. I was thinking I would take next quarter off to rest."

"I don't doubt you're tired, but a doctoral program is all about momentum. You have to go back to school. I've seen too many students think, 'oh, I'll just take a quarter off,' but never come back and finish their degree."

"But I really need rest."

And I did feel very tired, but he knew me well by that point. "How much is tuition for a quarter?"

"$7,000," I said, thinking about how much money that still felt like. I had been in the US for about three years, and I did not feel nearly as poor as I had when I arrived, but I still remembered making $7 a month in China. Although, to be fair, in China my housing, medical care, and much of my food was all paid for by the state.

I knew what he was going to say next, and I was right: "I'll send you a check."

By then his generosity was a familiar thing, but it never really became easier to accept, so "You don't have to do that," I protested. "I can pay for it."

"I think part of the reason you feel exhausted," he said, "is that you're so stressed out about the fact that you have to keep coming up with all this money. I'll pay for this quarter, and you'll get a break from the worry."

"Thank you," I said. "You take such good care of me. I will pay you back."

"That's fine. There's no hurry. Please don't worry about it—that would defeat the point!" He chuckled, and I had to smile.

So he mailed me a check for $7000, and I paid the tuition and continued my schooling. I was so touched! Dr. Rife really was my guardian angel. Without his support, I'm not sure if I would have made it through the program. Most likely not. When I started teaching at Georgetown College, probably three or four years later, it made such a difference for us financially; we no longer had to pay for my school and I was making a lot more money. So we saved up $10,000 and that year, right before Christmas, I mailed Dr. Rife a check and told him that we wanted to give him a big Christmas gift. Then the next spring he told me that he and his wife went to France, and flew first class, and I was very happy for them.

Several years into my Ph.D., during the long Memorial Day weekend, we went back to Indiana, PA to visit friends. The drive took us four hours, but when we were only halfway, our little red car broke down in the middle of the road. It was a Friday afternoon. We did not have AAA, and of course we did not know anyone nearby. Because we were on a highway and between towns, there were no pay phones. Since it was 1997, we had never heard of a cell phone, and even if we had, the only ones available were large and expensive.

So the only thing we could think to do was to ask for help to call the police. I would have to do it, even though I was nervous at the idea, because my English was much better than my husband's. It was not his fault; I worked closely with English speakers every day, and he did not, so I had much more practice.

We were on the big interstate highway, so I had to walk to an exit in order to find a phone. We had just passed Wheeling, West Virginia, and I was glad I did not have to walk much more than a mile to the last exit. When I got to the end of the exit ramp, I looked around. All I saw was a gas station and a Dairy Queen. I decided to try the Dairy Queen and hope to find a helpful employee, so I walked inside and went to the counter.

"Welcome to Dairy Queen," said the middle-aged woman behind the counter. "What can we get you today?"

"I'm sorry," I said, "I do not want to order anything. My car broke down, and I need to call for help." I felt nervous as I spoke, wondering whether she would understand my English; I knew my accent was strong. I also worried that she would not want to help.

"Oh dear, I'm sorry you're havin' trouble. Let me talk to my manager and see what we can do."

"Thank you." I watched her walk away and wondered how she was going to describe me. I felt out of place, so I decided to look at the other customers instead. As I said, I like to wonder where people are going, and a fast food restaurant along a highway seemed like a good place to do that. I also thought about my husband, who was waiting with the car, not knowing where I had gone or what was happening to me. I did not want him to worry, but of course I had little control over how long it would take.

The woman returned a few minutes later. "Sure, hon. You can use the phone in the office. Just go around to the left there, like you're goin' to the bathroom, and go on in the first door on the left."

I went where she was pointing, and found the door she had described. I did not feel comfortable just "going on in," so I knocked.

I was surprised to see a young man open the door. Somehow I always seem to expect senior personnel to be older than the junior ones.

"Sorry to hear you got car trouble, ma'am. Come on in."

"Thank you." I stepped in, and he gestured to the phone on his desk—which was a mess.

"Pardon the mess," he said apologetically, and turned the chair around for me to sit in. "Any idea who you're gonna call?"

"I don't know anyone here, so I was going to call the police."

"Well, you don't want to dial 911. I can recommend a tow truck if you want. Or I can get you the police non-emergency number."

I thought for a moment. Dr. Rife often told me I gave up too easily on what I wanted. So, "Thank you, I would like that police number please," I said.

He pulled a sheet of paper off the wall and handed it to me. "It's right there." He pointed to a line on the paper.

"Thank you." I sat down and dialed the number. The police officer I spoke to was very kind, and said they would arrange for our car to be towed to a body shop, but an officer would have to meet us at our car, to make sure it was the right one. I thanked him and hung up.

I handed the paper back to the young man and stood up. "I appreciate your kindness," I said. "I feel much better having a police officer involved."

"No problem, ma'am. Glad we could help. How far is your car?"

I hesitated, not knowing what sort of answer he was expecting.

"You walked here, right?" he asked.

"Yes. It was about twenty minutes of walking." Then I figured out what he was thinking. "I'll be okay, thanks."

"Okay, if you're sure. I could probably find someone to give you a ride if you wanted."

I shook my head. "Thank you, but it's no trouble to walk."

"Well, best of luck to you." He stuck out his hand, so I shook it and left.

As I walked back to my husband and son and our poor little car, I was happy that my search for a phone had gone so well. My husband gave me a big hug when I got there, obviously relieved to see me. A few minutes later a police car arrived. The officer quickly confirmed that I had made the call, then called a repair shop who could tow our car.

I guess it was a small business, because the owner himself drove the tow truck.

"Where you folks from?" he asked after introducing himself.

"Indiana, Pennsylvania," I answered.

"That's what, another couple hours away?"

We nodded.

"Thing is, it's almost four, and I'll be closing soon, and with the holiday on Monday, I won't get to your car till Tuesday."

My husband and I looked at each other with dismay. We had nowhere to stay over the weekend, especially with Chris—who of course had wanted to come with us to see his grandpa.

"We have nowhere to stay," I told him. "I know you want to close for the weekend, and I am sorry to trouble you, but is there any way you could work on our car now? I do not know what we will do until Tuesday without our car."

"Maybe it will be easy to fix," my husband added.

The owner looked us over. I think he felt sorry for us, two awkward Chinese immigrants who were completely out of place in rural West Virginia.

"I'll take a look," he said. We were so grateful to him. He took us in his tow truck—squeezed into the front seat—to his shop, and got to work. While we waited, we tried to decide what to do. Should we call someone and ask them to pick us up? Should we go back to Columbus, or go on to Indiana as we had planned? And if a friend did pick us up, would they be able to drive two hours again on Tuesday so we could get our car? We decided to call Dr. Rife to see what he thought we should do. He knew us well, and usually had good advice. The shop owner let us use his office phone.

"You say you're not in a town?" he asked after we had explained what happened.

"I don't think so," I answered. "There is a sign for a town, so maybe it is nearby. I can ask."

"No, don't bother. I was thinking that generally, one thing people do in that kind of situation is to get a motel room, but even if someone local gave you a ride to one, you can't really afford it. Especially since you're probably going to have a repair bill for your car."

"Right." It certainly hadn't occurred to us to stay at a motel.

"So don't worry. I'll pick you up. Meanwhile, when you find out what's wrong with the car, if you feel that you can't afford to fix it, ask if you can sell it to them. I'll take you to buy another one this weekend."

Wow. Even for Dr. Rife, this seemed like too much. It was not just that he was being generous with his money, which he had always done, but that he was also being generous with his time. To take more than four hours out of his day, just like that. . . .

"Thank you, thank you, thank you," was all I could think to say.

"What?" my husband asked, since he could only hear my side of the conversation.

"He says we can sell the car, and he will take us to buy another one."

"No, no, that is too much. Tell him we cannot accept."

"It's okay," I reassured him. "Dr. Rife genuinely wants to help out of love. He would be very hurt if we said no. Besides, what else would we do?"

My husband did not say anything, but his expression told me he would accept Dr. Rife's help.

Neither of us said anything for a few minutes after I hung up the phone.

The shop owner walked in from the garage. I could tell by the look on his face that he did not have good news.

"Sorry, folks, I can fix this, but it'll take me a couple weeks and cost you a lot of money."

"How much?"

"Maybe twenty-five hundred." He must have seen the unhappy looks on our faces. "I'll let you think it over. Just give a holler when you decide." He walked back into the garage.

I looked at my husband. "We only have $2,000."

"I guess we have to do what Dr. Rife said."

I thought about Becca and Eddie, who had given us the car for free after another car smashed into the driver's door. At first I felt like we had broken the gift they had so kindly given us, but then I thought, why would it be better if we had spent money on the car and could no longer use it? Becca and Eddie had been such good friends. They might be sad that we had to go through this, but I could not imagine them being upset because the car was ruined. Still, there were other questions to consider.

"If we spend our $2,000 on another car, we will have no savings," I said.

"If we don't spend it, we will have no car."

"We didn't have a car before."

"Do you want to go back to living like that?" my husband asked.

I had already started to think about that question. We had gotten by, of course. Walking a lot, taking busses, and getting rides from friends. It had all been part of feeling terribly poor. If we went back to that, after making progress, it might feel even worse than it had before—to lose something we had, compared to never having it in the first place. And Chris was older now. He had friends and school activities. I did not want to have to do all that without a car.

While it made me nervous to give up the savings we had worked so hard for, I said, "No."

"Good," he said. "Neither do I!" He went to the door to the garage, and called out,

"Hello?"

"Just a moment," came the owner's voice. "Gotta wipe off my hands."

He did walk back in a moment later, wiping his hands on a cloth. "What'll it be?"

"We would like to sell the car to you," I said.

His eyebrows went up in surprise. "Sell it to me? I'm not an auto dealer, you know."

"You could use it for parts."

He looked at me thoughtfully. "I'm guessing you can't afford to fix it."

We nodded. "I am sorry. But if you buy it, you can save money on parts, right?"

He stopped to consider. "Sure. There are plenty of Nissans around, so that should work. And hey, it's not like you have tons of options."

We were so grateful. "Thank you!" We both said.

"The tow was forty bucks. How much you wanna sell for?"

"Well . . . " I looked at my husband. "We did not pay anything for it, so we do not expect to make money selling it." He nodded in agreement.

"How about we call it fifty bucks," the owner said.

I looked at my husband again, and he shrugged as if to say it was okay with him.

So we paid him, and signed over the title. Then we just needed to get our luggage out of the car, and wait for Dr. Rife.

It was a strange feeling. I suppose that because we did not pay for the car, it had always felt a bit like we were just borrowing it from Becca and Ed. Now we had sold it to a stranger in West Virginia, and Dr. Rife . . . it was not always Dr. Rife to the rescue. As I have talked about, there have been many people who helped us over the years. Dr. Rife is just the one who so often went beyond what we could ever have thought someone would do for us. But that made me think of something—

"I do not know," I said to my husband, "exactly what Dr. Rife had in mind when he said he would take us to buy another car. I hope he does not mean to pay for it."

"No, we must insist on paying for it!" he said. "We have money. He does not need to pay."

That made sense to me too.

I was so happy to see Dr. Rife when he drove up, I gave him a big hug. He checked in with the shop owner to make sure that we were all done, then drove us to Indiana. On the way, I reflected on what it had taken for us to get there: the kindness of two strangers—the Dairy Queen manager and the repair shop owner—and a degree of kindness that was remarkable from a man I already knew to be remarkably kind.

Then that weekend, as he had said he would, Dr. Rife took us out to shop for a car. We went to several places, and found a red Ford we liked, but it was $4,000. It was a nice car, we just did not have that much money.

Since we had prepared for this moment, I said, "We need to find one we can afford."

"But you really like this one," he said.

"I'm sorry," my husband blurted out, "we cannot let you buy it for us."

I felt a bit embarrassed, but he did not know Dr. Rife as well as I did, and I did not blame him for being worried about it.

Dr. Rife just laughed. "Fair enough," he said. "Would you let me loan you the extra money, so you can get a car you really like?"

I had not considered that possibility. I conferred with my husband, and we agreed that was okay. So together we bought the car; Dr. Rife paid for it, since otherwise we would have owed money to the bank and had to pay interest—if they had given us a loan, which they might not have done since we had no credit history.

One thing surprised me, though. I took Dr. Rife aside. "Why didn't you bargain? You just paid the $4,000 on the sticker. Everyone tells me you are supposed to bargain when you buy a car."

"I'm sorry." He looked embarrassed. "I've never figured out how to haggle. It's so uncomfortable, and I don't know the rules. So I just don't."

I found that curious. Dr. Rife seemed like such a capable man in so many ways; it had never occurred to me that something as simple as bargaining would be beyond him. But I did not think any less of him, since everyone has flaws.

After the weekend we drove the new car back home. That was our second car. From that time on, we paid Dr. Rife maybe two or three hundred dollars per month until one day he said, that's enough. We never counted, actually.

After my son graduated from college, he went to work on Wall Street, first at JP Morgan, then at Deutsche Bank. Recently he quit his job and

Figure 12.1.   Color photograph of IUP Oak Grove. From Keith Boyer/Indiana University of Pennsylvania

organized a startup company with one of his friends from work. Now they have more than forty people working for them. They are doing very well—more on that later. I mention this because for quite a while, every time we went to visit Dr. Rife, he took us out for lunch or dinner. Finally one time we had finished eating dinner, but before he had a chance to pay the bill, Chris paid. I didn't expect that! It was so funny to see the grandson pay for the meal instead of the grandfather as was usual. We jokingly said to Chris, he is a banker now, and he has a fat wallet, so he should pay from now on.

Chapter Thirteen

Guests in this World

We moved to Columbus, Ohio in the summer of 1993. It was a much bigger city than Indiana, and while I think the whole metropolitan area was about the size of Pittsburgh's, the city of Columbus itself was much bigger. And being the state capital gave it extra importance. The Ohio State University, of course, is quite a large university, but coming from Indiana where the student population was as large as the resident population, the city dwarfed the university. It certainly proved to be a better place for my husband to do business. The fact that the city was located at the confluence of two rivers reminded me of Luoyang, but it still took me a while to adjust to living in such a larger city.

For the first several years there, we lived in an area that was pretty shabby, simply because that was where we could afford to live. But since most of the residents were international students, we became good friends with two neighboring families from China, the Nis (who I mentioned earlier) and the Jiangs. Mrs. Ni was an expert at managing money, both by saving and by keeping their expenses down—as I said, they shared an apartment with another family, the Jias and did not even use heat in winter. She saved a lot of money, at least what we considered a lot at the time. It helped that they had a stable income, but she followed the saying, "a penny saved is a penny earned." I think we were the poorest among all the people we knew from China. Their daughter is now a medical doctor, and they moved to Canada a few years before we left Columbus.

Mrs. Ni sometimes criticized me; she would say things like, "you should learn how to save money—a poor peasant does not live like a rich landlord." I certainly did not think I was living like a rich landlord! I have never liked to go shopping for clothing, shoes, jewelry, and bags like so many women. But it is true that I am no good at figuring out where and how to save money on this and that. I should learn from her.

At that time, my husband was trying to start a new business, but we had no money for it. He had studied what to do, and we decided to ask the Nis if we could borrow $3,000 from them. They were happy to do it, which was so generous. Looking back at it now, I do not know how they thought we would pay them back, since we were so poor. But they trusted us, and my husband did eventually make some money using the $3,000. Of course we worked hard to pay them back, and we paid them more than they lent us; they had not asked us to, or charged us interest, but it was a good way to express our gratitude.

Just before the Nis moved to Canada, we invited them and the Jiangs to dinner at a good restaurant. It was not actually a very expensive restaurant, but we wanted to treat them to the meal and it cost about $100. We only had a little more than $100 in our bank account, but my husband expected to make a deal soon, and we thought we would shortly have more money. So we took a chance and paid for the entire meal, even though it was all our money. It was that important to us to show them how much we appreciated their trust and friendship.

After settling into Columbus, we decided to get a credit card, but of course we had no credit history at all. When we went to the bank, they would not give us a card. They said our only option was to apply for a secured credit card, which means you put money into an account, and then you can spend that much on your credit card. It keeps you from spending more money than you have. So we did that, putting $1,000 into the account. The bank told us that after a year we should be eligible for a real credit card, but after a year they still did not give us one. Several more years passed before we finally did. Now we get credit card offers in the mail every day, and the credit line on our card is higher than we could ever have dreamed it would be.

We tried to save money by getting things for free whenever we could. One big church in Columbus would give away free furniture and clothing once or twice a year. We also went to a lot of yard sales, of course. We got many our things from those places, and even now, I keep some of it because it reminds me of that time. Once we stopped at a yard sale, and as I wandered through it, I found two pairs of jeans that looked nice, and I thought Chris could wear them. But when I went to buy them, the owner said, "Those are girls' jeans." I think I still bought them, and wound up sending them to my niece in China. Later on, we started going to the Macy's basement sale.

My husband went through a number of business ideas over the years. He would try something for a while, see how well it worked, and then move on to a new one if the old one did not work as well as he hoped. One time, I pointed out to him that he could cut out all the middlemen in the business he had been running, and start a new one by working directly with the original seller. I had a whole vision for it, and he liked it. Eventually we did find the original seller, in southern China—this was a different company than I talked about in the first half—and we were able to make up to $10,000 a year for the next several years. That helped us to buy our first new car, a white Corolla. It was a basic car that did not even have cruise control, which we wanted. We paid the dealership an extra hundred dollars to add it, and they did, but most of the time it did not work. Eventually we bought a much fancier car, a Toyota SUV that was fully loaded. We have always bought Toyotas.

In 1996, when Chris was in 5th grade, we moved to a much nicer part of Columbus because the school was the best in the entire city. We were still renting an apartment, but all the homes nearby were beautiful stone or brick single houses. While I did enjoy the area more, mostly we were happy that Chris could go to a better school. He stayed in that school system through his first year of high school, when we moved to Lexington.

As I said, once Chris learned to read, he read a lot, which makes me happy. There was one downside to all the reading: he thought he knew enough words. His senior year in high school, I bought an SAT practice for him, but he refused to read it.

He said, "No, Mom, I can't just recite the dictionary."

But I did not see him studying. So two weeks before the SAT he was scheduled to take, I came back from a conference, and my husband and I staged a conversation for Chris to hear; we waited till he was in another room, close enough to overhear us.

"I met some professors at the conference," I started, "from schools like Harvard and Columbia, so I asked them about their academic standards for the students they admitted."

"You mean like SAT scores?" my husband asked. "What did they say?"

"Well, I was surprised to hear most of them say that it depended on the group of people."

"They didn't just have one standard they applied to everyone?"

"No, but it wasn't because they expected different things of different groups. It was because they can't let everyone in, even from a group like Asian students, and different groups tend to perform at different levels."

"So if they used a certain standard for one group, it might let in the right number of people from that group, but too many from another group?"

"Right."

"What do they look for from Asian students?" he asked.

"They said male Asian students had to have at least a 1300 SAT score, out of 1600. But they also said most of the Asian kids they accepted had scores of 1550 or higher. It is very competitive. And it is graded on a scale, so if you have a high score, missing one question loses many more points than if you have a low score and miss one question."

"Then you really have to work hard," my husband said, "if you want to get the highest score."

"That's what they said."

Then I changed the subject, because that was the main point I wanted to get across. And it worked. Later that day, Chris came to me with the practice book.

"There are 140 pages of vocabulary," he said, "so if I study ten pages a day, I'll finish before the test."

I was stunned. I thought to myself, oh my God, I couldn't even do that after so many years of studying English. I had looked through the SAT book, and although I had been studying, teaching, and speaking English for about fifteen years, I did not know 90% of the vocabulary. How could he learn that much in fourteen days?

But after twelve days he came to me and said, "I finished all these words. I already knew most of them."

I was so shocked. "How did you do that?"

"I guess I have a good long-term memory for words. I just study the word, and then it's locked in my memory. I still remember all the words I learned five or six years ago."

I was so glad to hear that.

Two days later he took the exam, and he got a full score on the vocabulary section. He almost got a perfect score on the math section as well, and ended up with a total score of 1560 / 1600. He wasn't surprised since he knew all the words in the exams.

When I have younger friends with children, I tell them, let your kids read, and read more, and their memory will get better and better.

Chris played the violin, and he got quite good at it that he was accepted by the Youth Orchestra of Greater Columbus and, after we moved, the Central Kentucky Youth Orchestra. He also learned to draw and paint. I mentioned that he played lacrosse in middle and high school, and when we moved, he ended up playing with the city's lacrosse club since the high school he went to didn't have a lacrosse team. His high school CV looked excellent, and helped him get into the University of Chicago to study economics.

As I said, Chris felt very sad when it was time to leave Columbus. He had actually been staying with a friend for a month. He had a summer class to finish, and the house we had bought in Lexington needed work, so my husband and I rented an apartment for that month. We thought it would be better for Chris to stay in Columbus that month, and that was a good decision.

Despite how hard it was for him to say goodbye to his friends, it would have been worse if he had gone through that and then been stuck with us in an apartment in a new city with no friends and not even school to go to. And looking back on it, the fact that his friends came running to say goodbye to him was a wonderful moment. It means a lot to me that he was able to make good friends like that after coming to a strange country.

I mentioned the time Dr. CS gave me the only C in the class, then refused to give me feedback on a paper, and sent a memo about that C grade to all my professors. By that point I was the only student from China still in the class, because all the others had dropped it after the first week. Maybe I would have too, but I was his Ph.D. student and could not. Anyway, a few years later I ran into him in the history department hallway; he had retired by then, but was still active on campus in other ways. For instance, many students also knew his wife because she taught piano, and he served as master of ceremonies for the annual piano recital.

"Miss He!" he called out. "May I speak to you for a moment?"

"Of course," I said.

"Several years ago, I gave you a C on a test, and treated you badly afterward. I am very sorry I did that. I was wrong to do it."

"Thank you, I appreciate that."

"You must continue your studies, and move forward. Don't let me become an obstacle in your life."

I was very touched by his honesty, and by the courage it took for him to do that. It was not even the last time he mentioned it, either. After he retired and I was teaching at Georgetown College, I received a letter from him at Christmas. Of course it had a holiday greeting and updates from his family, but he once again apologized. He wrote something like, *the world was yours now, I already stepped down and was just a guest having a great time in your world.* I was even more touched this time by his warmth, integrity, and optimism. Dr. CS, you were wrong. We are all guests in this world. Someday, all of us will leave.

When he passed away in 2013, I received a letter from the department asking me to write a memorial about him. He had done so much to make up for how he behaved at first, which I was honored by the request and did write something in memory of him. I talked about how he had recruited me into the Chinese history Ph.D. program in 1993. And I talked about that second letter, and how I thought he was wrong. May Dr. CS rest in peace in heaven.

Sometimes it was difficult to have students from Taiwan and from mainland China in the same classes, talking about the People's Republic of China—especially when the professor had his own bias. Dr. CH did not like mainland China at all. It was not surprising since the Communists had imprisoned his father in law and let everyone think he was dead. Dr. CH did not talk about it publicly, but he also did not always keep discussions balanced as he could have. In one of his seminars, with a mix of Chinese students like I said, some students attacked China's policies on women's rights. It was easy for Taiwanese and American students to do, because they can only compare the situation in China to what they have experienced. The other students and I from the mainland felt very uncomfortable during that class, because I had only been in this country for three years and was still heavily influenced by life under the CCP.

That night I talked it over with another student who felt the way I did.

"Chairman Mao said 'Women hold up half the sky'!" she said, scowling. "I don't see how anyone can find fault with that."

"Well, you know that his sayings often had a political motive behind them, and were often not consistent with his policies, and it is the policies that were attacked in class," I pointed out.

"But he did so much to improve the lives of women! He eliminated prostitution—can Americans say that?"

"No, you're right, and women would never have held positions of power in Imperial China."

I watched her indignation, and thought about how the students in class had clearly felt. "I think it is a matter of perspective. We see the glass half full, because we know how far China has come, but the other students only see the difference that exists now, so they see the glass half empty."

I could not sleep that night because I could not stop thinking about it. I wound up writing down a lot of questions I wanted to discuss with Dr. CH. So the next day I went to his office during office hours, and told him why I was there—about the discomfort I and other mainland Chinese students had felt in yesterday's class. He let me ask my questions, and he had a lot to say about them. He did most of the talking, but I did get through all my questions.

Finally he said, "I'm just a human being, and I make mistakes. If something like this happens again, if I make another mistake in class, point it out immediately so everyone can benefit."

I was quite happy with how that turned out.

Despite how hopeless I felt at Ohio State that I would ever find a teaching job in Chinese history, it actually went well. The last two years of my Ph.D. program I was working on my dissertation. I mentioned how, even after I finished it and had started my new job at Georgetown College, I had to go back to Ohio State to defend my dissertation. Despite the drama with it being cancelled, I was able to get the committee together and do the defense, and I passed. In fact, everybody said it was excellent. I worked on it over the years, rewriting and revising, and in December of 2012 the State University of New York (SUNY) Press published it as *Red Genesis: The Hunan First Normal School and the Creation of Chinese Communism, 1903-1921.*

I started looking for a job in the first year of my dissertation work. I did not make much progress that year, but the second year I wound up with fourteen interviews. Of course I had never done real job interviews before, and I know a lot of Americans who feel very nervous doing them, so I did not do well on the first couple interviews. But I did get better at them. I had one interview in Boston, and I really wanted that job. I was the first of three candidates they interviewed, but the department chair left for England right after my interview, so they told me the other two interviews would be done when he returned.

The next week I went to my interview at Georgetown College near Lexington, Kentucky, for the position of Assistant Professor of Asian history. I had never heard of Lexington before I applied for this job at Georgetown. I thought Kentucky was beautiful. It had more forest and fewer fields, like central Pennsylvania only with fewer people. Georgetown College is actually in a suburb of Lexington named Georgetown, about nine miles north.

While the Lexington metropolitan area is much smaller than either Pittsburgh or Columbus, the city proper is about as big as Pittsburgh; I was surprised to discover that.

Lexington has been growing, and the traffic is horrible during the rush hour, but otherwise it has been a good place to live. There are a number of universities and colleges aside from Georgetown, and the city seems to value education. It is the perfect environment, given my family background, but also an ironic one, given that I grew up during a time when academics were reviled.

Anyway, my interview went on for two days and ended on a late Friday afternoon, and since it was only a three hour drive, I went home that evening. Early the next morning—a Saturday—the department chair called me to say, "Everyone voted for you, so the job is yours." I had a good impression of them too. I decided that Georgetown was my academic home. Since academic etiquette says that you have to respond to a job offer within a week, I could not wait until the department chair at the college in Boston returned. Actually, I had fourteen campus visit offers that year. University of Rochester offered me to teach two courses per semester the first year only after phone interview (see how good I was at interviews at that time), yet I declined their offer without hesitation.

So I have been teaching at Georgetown College since 2001. The department chair who hired me became a close friend, and later on when the school began to struggle financially, he apologized several times for "dragging me into this." But I feel fortunate to work there. My colleagues are good friends, the students are thoughtful and respectful, and my neighbors are so friendly and helpful. Lexington has been our home since then, and I still love teaching as much as I did when I started at Luoyang Teachers' College in 1982. Looking back, it is hard to believe it took me ten years to get back to teaching! Teaching is my passion. A main reason for me to choose college teaching as my profession is that I see the promise that lies in contributing to the intellectual and personal development of students, and to the transformation of students into complete persons.

I am a historian. The excitement of a historian's life, I always believe, lies in his or her potential to advance moral values and promote the common good.

Chris showed an interest in business early on in life, and did well with a small business selling various products on eBay by the time he was in high school.

The summer after his junior year at the University of Chicago, he interned in the investment banking division of a major, "bulge bracket" bank headquartered in New York, and they offered him a job at the end of the summer.

So when he graduated with a major in Economics in June of 2008, he was ready to begin working on Wall Street right away. However, this was a turbulent time in history and the Great Financial Crisis of 2007-2008 was well underway.

The bank he was to join had just acquired a distressed competitor, and decided to defer half of its new investment banking analyst class to join the following year.

Chris was crestfallen when he was given the news of his deferral less than a month before he was to start, and decided to take their offer of working temporarily in a financial planning department for a year before starting with the class of 2009.

This was a low point in Chris's life. He had been swept up in the bull market fervor of the mid-2000's and had bought into the propaganda of Wall Street's incredibly effective recruiting machine.

Instead of working on Wall Street as he imagined, he received an early lesson in humility and worked in a "middle office" position in New York for a year. Even though he was based in one of the bank's main office towers in Midtown Manhattan, it was a small department filled by mostly older employees that had stayed in the same role for decades with whom he shared few interests with.

It was a difficult year for him personally as none of his friends from college were in New York, and he didn't have a new analyst class of potential friends to make. He rented an apartment with two colleagues from his intern class who hadn't been deferred, but they worked long hours and he rarely saw them. At one point, Chris resorted to playing computer games in his free time for months on end.

After that year ended, the bank kept its promise and Chris started with the investment banking analyst class of 2009. Even though he liked many of the analysts from his training class, ironically he quickly found out that he hated the job. Perhaps it had a little to do with him being placed in a new industry group, but regardless, he abhorred the "cubicle culture" and the office politics that came with the job. He sometimes worked 100 hours a week, and even had to sleep under his desk a few nights for just a few hours.

The worst part was that he felt that he simply wasn't that good at a job that he instinctively did not like. He could do the Excel models and check a presentation twenty times before handing it up to the next layer in the hierarchy, but he knew in his heart that something was wrong. He felt lost as the two year program progressed and his fellow analysts followed the path laid out for them and received offers at private equity firms.

As his two year contract as an investment banking analyst was coming to an end, Chris was at a crossroads without an offer to continue at the bank nor a job offer from a private equity firm or hedge fund.

It's rare to know from the beginning what you want to do in life, and more likely, you'll have to try a few things to learn what you don't like, in order to get closer to discovering what you want to do and who you wish to be.

As it turns out, Chris was contacted by a recruiter one day about an opportunity to work on the trading floor in New York at a major European bank with a deep presence in the Americas. He met with several senior executives from the structured finance department with whom he instantly bonded, and ironically became the first analyst in his investment banking group to leave, two months before the end of his two year analyst contract.

Chris was much happier on the trading floor. The work was a better fit for him, and the culture valued performance much more than how well he played office politics. He did well. He was one of the best performers in the structured finance department and was considered a rising star. I think he had a sharp eye for commercial opportunities, or a "commercial nose" as his manager liked to say.

He initially had a more senior partner with whom he worked on deals with whom Chris liked a lot, and they always looked out for each other. However, one day and very unexpectedly, his senior partner was laid off. When it came time to transition deals and clients to other senior executives, all of Chris and his partner's clients wanted to stay with Chris. As a result, Chris ended up becoming a senior contributor much faster than expected, and in his first year as a Vice President he brought in over $25 million in revenue for the firm.

Even though Chris had been deferred a year, he made it up on the trading floor. He left two months early in his second year as an Analyst and joined the new bank as an Associate. And because he joined in April of 2011 as an Associate, he only spent one year and eight months as an Associate before being promoted to Vice President at the start of 2013.

However, Chris knew it was time for a change after bonus season came around in February 2014. He felt that the environment had become increasingly un-meritocratic and political. Despite producing a personal record amount of revenue, his total compensation did not increase accordingly.

He knew that he needed to make a change, because if he stayed still, they would just continue to pay him the least that they could get away with year after year.

At first, he thought that his "Plan A" would be to move to the private wealth division of the bank and to partner with a private banker he had worked with to sell structured products and other esoteric investments to ultra high net worth investors. At the time, private banking was one of the few areas left in finance where there was still a degree of merit based pay.

His "Plan B" was to start a business of his own. He first moonlighted by working at an events company he started with a couple of acquaintances, more to start something just for the sake of starting something. He quickly realized after a few months that it wouldn't have legs, and he exited the partnership.

But by then, he had a new business partner, a colleague who sat next to him on the trading floor and whom he frequently grabbed lunch with. One day in August 2014, they were brainstorming over lunch and decided to go into business together.

For a few months after that, he was still employed at the bank but was coming into the office less and less. Plan A was still to join the private bank while his new business was still in its infancy.

However, life sometimes makes a move on you, such that you are forced to confront your destiny. As it turned out, the bank first asked him to take a paid leave of absence until the new position at the private bank could be sorted out. But then in January 2015 while he was on his paid leave, he got a call telling him that there would be no job at the private bank, and that he was being laid off.

With Plan A now out of the realm of possibility, Chris was forced to make something out of nothing, to find a way out of no way. It was tough at first. In their first full year of operation they only generated about $10,000 in revenue. We were fortunate to be in a position to be able to help support him during those tough early years, and we are proud of the sacrifices Chris and his business partner made to keep living and operating expenses to a minimum.

After many important lessons and countless iterations, the company started to take off. Eventually, the initial idea evolved into multiple brands, becoming one of the largest players in the NYC metro area. Chris and his business partner now run a successful, multi-million dollar business with over 60 team members as of this writing.

Chris always liked to say that everything happens for a reason. As it turns out, he met the love of his life on his 28th birthday. He threw an

Figure 13.1.   Color photograph of the Statue of Liberty. From William T. McCabe

enormous party for that birthday and often describes it as the peak of his bachelor days. The party ended early by chance, and it was also by chance that he decided to meet up for some friends that evening, and the rest is history.

Chris had always doubted that he would ever be able to meet a quality woman he could settle down with in a city that moves as fast as New York. However, life is full of surprises.

Chris is now settled down and happily married with a beautiful, smart, driven, funny and elegant young lady from Sweden.

When I came to this country as a poor Chinese immigrant, I would never have believed that my son could do so well. He is prospering both personally and financially, and I could not be more proud.

I have been on leave from Georgetown College for three years, and my husband and I are living in New York during this time. Every night, as our workout, we go for a fast walk along the Hudson River. Sometimes we walk all the way down to Battery Park, and whenever we do that, I look out at the Statue of Liberty and think of Emma Lazarus's sonnet:

> Give me your tired, your poor,
> Your huddled masses yearning to breathe free,
> The wretched refuse of your teeming shore.
> Send these, the homeless, tempest-tost to me,
> I lift my lamp beside the golden door!

I feel so moved by this symbol of America, so grateful to this great country and to those beautiful people I have encountered. You opened your arms, accepted us, and gave us opportunities to prove that we are worth it.